The Crumbling Mansion

Also by Charles Freyberg and published by Ginninderra Press
Dining at the Edge

Charles Freyberg

The Crumbling Mansion

Deepest thanks to Peter Urquhart, Judith Beveridge, Tim Wright, Lou Steer, Candy Royalle, Deirdre Freyberg, Stephen and Brenda Matthews, Marguerite Montes, Alison Marshall, Angela Stretch, Sarah Gilbert, John O'Driscoll, Mary Burgess, Troy Davies, Victor Sheehan, Charlotte Jasmine Black, Danny Gentile, Vashti Hughes, Aaron Manhattan, Hugh Monroe, Luke Rogers, Vittorio Bianchi and friends at the Picolo Café, Danny Gardner, Tug Dumbly, Kerri Shying, Dimitra Harvey, Richard Short, Gregory Dickerson, Marjorie McIntosh, Jo Northey, Mia Mortal, the poets of the University of Sydney Graduate Seminar, the poets of Word in Hand.

Written on Gadigal and Gundangara land, energised by 60,000 years of continuous storytelling

The Crumbling Mansion
ISBN 978 1 76109 172 8
Copyright © Charles Freyberg 2021
Cover painting by Victor Sheehan
Author drawing by Tristan Franki

First published 2021 by
GINNINDERRA PRESS
PO Box 3461 Port Adelaide 5015
www.ginninderrapress.com.au

Contents

Introduction	7
Forest Elegy	9
To Victor	13
Essay on Shakespeare	14
The Mirror	16
Amber Hands	17
A Cold Sweat on the Lawn	20
First Impressions	23
I Am Not Dostoyevsky	25
Boarding House	28
Cat	29
You Draw Me	30
Endgame	32
Nightclub	34
Boom	36
Fathers	37
Maze	40
The street unravels	43
Bonfire of Barristers	45
Another Walk	46
My Clown	48
Trickster Spirit	50
Performance	52
Angel	54
Schooner	57
Focus	60
The Captain	63
Angel of Death	67

Victoria Street: A Kings Cross Fantasia 1973	69
I: Helen	70
II: Tony and Vanessa	90
III: Michael	100
IV: Louise and Vanessa	115
V: After Dinner	129
Terrania Creek Revisited	138
After the Bushfire	140
Regeneration	142
Rain at Rosebank	144
Coachwood Glen	145
Echidna	150
Banksia	152
Albarracin Fantasia	155
Altarpiece Saint Mary's Krakow	157
Warsaw Square	160
Warsaw Gay Bar	162
To Candy Royalle	163
Notes	164
About the Author	167

Introduction

What is going on inside Charles's poetry is a continuous representation of the primal dynamic of life. Charged with high sensuality, drama, exclamations and interrogations succeeding one another. Where he might have destroyed himself, his possession of the world is certain.

Angela Stretch

The Crumbling Mansion grapples with issues of identity and sexuality, with loneliness, grief and the power of the dead to suffuse our present. Freyberg's imagery is kaleidoscopic, sometimes hallucinatory; the speaker's senses – electric with the textures of the world – spark swirling sojourns into the imagination and memory – rendering time less linear and more porous.

What I admire most about Freyberg's collection is its theatricality and eroticism, its dauntless flamboyance which is an act of resistance. Freyberg centres bodies and desires that don't conform to society's bland, heteronormative binary; its claustrophobic renderings of femininity and masculinity, beauty and desirability. In the face of violence and bigotry, corruption and rapacity, Freyberg's motley crew of misfits, libertines, and pariahs – creatives and everyday revolutionaries – dare self-discovery and expression, acceptance of difference, kindness, gentleness.

Freyberg's nature poems reveal an eye that spans the microscopic details of moss, to the macroscopic vistas of mountain valleys. An eye that delights and luxuriates in the sensuousness of the more-than-human world.

Dimitra Harvey

Charles Freyberg describes the underbelly of Kings Cross that is known only by those who have trodden the path. Charles's strength as a performance poet is met by the power of his words on the page. His poetry stays in the mind after being read because of his dynamic and lyrical story telling as well as his vulnerability and fragility as he walks a road less travelled.

Vashti Hughes

Forest Elegy

Terrania Creek

I'm poised in my study
searching for a forest
in a scattering of notebooks
filled with sprawling biro,
repeating, refining
like variations on a violin,
a work without an end.
My dead friend's painting stares,
swirling lines of his satire brighten
the piano slows, the violin sprints
coloured folders open as layers of paper
start drifting in the breeze…

I got in a car.
I drove away.
Freeway, highway, town, fields
until a dirt road narrowing
led me to this towering forest.
I searched for a place to enter,
a chink, a path…

Leaves tumble down in somersaults
like brown moths tinged with green
a root rests like a tentacle
oozing with moss
fallen branches rot in shadow
the creek rushes and bubbles below.

A trunk is cut with furrows
each gnarl a tangle of splinters,
it splits at random angles
branches reach, splitting again
to a mesh of new leaves
gleaming with sunlight.

The violin meanders
frozen notes on paper writhe,
the painting swirls
a dead writer's bright anxiety,
a moment of shared laughter.

Circles are spinning on the pool,
expanding and vanishing
so quickly they're always there,
a hiss against the water whooshing
through jagged polished rocks.
I follow a tree's gigantic trunk
past staghorns, scars of branches lost
skipping shadows of leaves above.
A bird swoops out of layers of fern fronds
a whip cracks and echoes,
the frogs are burping raspberries.
And like a distant drumming,
the sound of the falls.

The forest voices are bubbling together
like choristers scattered far and wide,
wails, hums and basses
a language that cannot be spoken
but full of such patterns of feeling,
I begin to know what it's saying.
Circles are spinning on the pool
as I sense you beside me
whispering your fantasies,
slowly breathing like me…

A wisp of water glares
shattering to a spray
down the long mottled cliff
so quickly renewing
it shimmers in a frozen glow.
The pool bubbles around me
wrapped in layers of trees,
it's like I'm cupped in a gentle hand
reaching into weary muscles,
my skin is now transparent
my body spreads, caressed.
Loving to drift
I savour delight as long as I dare
ageless in my nakedness.

My notes sit calmly.
The hand behind the painting,
with all his quirks and tangents
quietly listens with me
as the violin skips high, then low.
This is my home.
My work is done.

To Victor

in memory of Victor Sheehan

The only copies of your plays
are sitting in a folder.
I'm frightened to read them.
They're relics
in an ancient typeface.
I'm still prickled by the broken shards
of your spontaneity,
the caress and jab of your irony.
Your voice is tangled in mine
enlivening my own work
waiting on the desk.
Years ago
I scattered your ashes,
scattered fantasies
still whispering in me now…

Essay on Shakespeare

It's finished.
I want to rip it in pieces.
I think I found
a strident tone
peppered with footnotes
veering with dry qualifications
with nothing of my howl,
this is me…

come ye spirits that tend on mortal thoughts
when in disgrace with fortune and…
To make an envious mountain on my back
Where sits deformity to mock my body…

but how to footnote a howl, a gasp,
nausea in Sydney 1984?
Not this or that professor
propped open on my desk…

A gentle hiss,
the boy down the hallway is showering…
I gasp.

Why compare and contrast
in a quiet clipped voice
a stifling mask
a smelly coffee-stained cardigan,
like my lecturer sighing?

A woman's face with Nature's own hand painted
hast thou the master/ mistress of my passion…
Wet footsteps in the corridor,
he's wrapped in a towel…
He'd slap me if I said that,
I'd slap him back
or share some turgid patter from my essay
or 'there's a keg on later, lots of chicks',
what can I say?
I have no voice,
no feelings at all.
My erection is unendurable.

A ciggie burns my lips,
I light another.
Time to start another essay –
T.S. Eliot the 'Waste Land'.
Let's drain the juices from another furious renegade.
April is the cruellest month
I prop open some new professors.
I howl.

The Mirror

I'm half a coddled schoolboy,
my legs now downed with hair
in a jumper knitted by my mother,
it shrouds my body
concealing my sex,
I cannot remove it.

A blemish on the mirror
cuts my body in two.

Above
sunlight on my glasses,
the smoke from my lips is dazzling,
the stain uncoils
to flecks jostling blue and orange
like make-up smoothing over
the pimple scars on my face.
My body is luminous,
a shadow with a shining corona,
I am changed.

Until the sun is swallowed by a cloud,
a breeze blows in the window.
I am a bespectacled boy
in a dirty jumper with no trousers
smoking a cigarette
looking for some hidden wonder
in my oh so familiar face.

Amber Hands

Amber hands
in purple flashing light
sinews twitch with echoing laughter –
at what? I'm always a step
behind their conspiracy.
Rippling muscles heat flanneled shirts
Love love me do in Waterloo
I have no breath to ignite my words
they catch in my throat as I scull,
I can decipher what they say, not what they mean,
have I forgotten my own language?
Deformed, unfinished, sent before my time
into this breathing world scarce half made up…
I can be their clown!
I rearrange their words in awkward parody
they grimace and cackle,
our schooners glow a frothy purple,
I want to flow with them,
a nerve aches in my brain
like a rotting tooth,
I want to cut it out,
as I see
a tree-lined street
floating high above our heads…

Is this what knits us together?
A house flashes purple in plastered brick,
a father and a mother tend to the crying child –
you're safe, you're loved, life is good –
turning all his fear to laughter,
he frolics, duck diving in a pool
no sorrow, no unravelling
no blinding light on the mirror.
Is this the place we all came from,
our anchor – or our leg iron?
A cocoon of plush cushions
languid couches, raucous barbecues –
you're a special boy, the dux, you'll be successful
life is good, you'll marry, find a tree-lined street.
Let's clink glasses, and stand together
grinning in an everlasting photo…
But the father sighs unnoticed
he holds his wife's hand,
I cannot see her face or body,
then the towel slips from her hips.
It's the boy from down the corridor!
His face distorts
shifting to a howling clown,
his body glows purple…

Faces are spinning,
the bar rattles and shouts
with the fixed smile of loveless love songs
until I see…
His eyes like mine staring inward –
hiding the secret of his virginity?
Words form, about to burst out
in thrilling spontaneity –
'I want to be anywhere but here
let's tear beneath the surface and find…'
I touch his hand and he recoils
his eyes now have *their* easy clarity
not veering away from the straight ahead,
he staggers, but with them…
Suddenly I'm alone
in glaring light
being swept away with a broom
with cigarette butts and stragglers.

A Cold Sweat on the Lawn

(University of Sydney, night time)

A cold sweat on the lawn
glistens green
in thickening shadows,
splintering bark of a tree trunk
pierces the fabric of my shirt,
putrid with half chewed lumps of vomit.
The scar of a lopped-off branch
grins at me like a gargoyle,
I wave back as it spins.
Street lights reach for the clouds,
layers of swirling greyness
shifting to the pitch above –
is this the emptiness,
the nothing inside me?
The stars are braided
in scorched ribbons,
traffic rumbles like the riff of a bass guitar.

My muscles flex
as I shift my twisted legs,
but the texture of my chest
beneath my unbuttoned shirt
is sweet – I caress myself.
A stammering boy
peels off his clothes –
the warmth of his body questioning –
'Do I dare?' – to stare
into swelling pockets of darkness
to find my completion,
my foul gorgeous toad
my vagabond.
I cannot be a fawning copy of the others,
poised to take over the world.
They walk past like shadows snickering,
not offering a helping hand.
I am here.
I am content.
A mist of drizzle falls
mixing with my smoke
the pungency of vomit,
I throw up again.

Beyond the trees
the fake Gothic towers are pinpricks.
Professors join hands
singing in a flat repeating chorus
ignoring the sarcasm of the sky.
I want to share these contradictions
with a fellow renegade –
Do I see this time
through the distorting prism of you?
Now I am ready to meet you.

First Impressions

His sneer cuts me,
his lips – are they rouged?
Powder hides the lines on his face.
Is he old – or younger than me?
He wears a battered hat.
Other students snicker
with their flawless skin, a blank cool
but he lets out a raucous laugh.
I'm laughing too – with him, at him?
My inner scholar stiffens,
I swivel my head for guidance.
The others twitch uncomfortably
and I do too, as he reads from his play,
spewing out images in jagged tangents
a rollicking rhythm in a dark kiwi twang,
spilling garbage on my tree-lined street.

The shopping mall smells of disinfectant
as politicians with crinkle cut hairdos
cut up babies…
What? 'What nonsense he talks!'
I say in my most measured voice,
recoiling from his playful fury.
The others disappear
but I walk up for a closer look
and offer my hand
as he explodes with laughter again.

He sees I'm shaking.
I want nothing to do with him.
I'm a model student.
My life is free of all this darkness!
As I turn to leave, he smiles
and asks me to visit him.
Do I want to know more?

I Am Not Dostoyevsky

As the piano sprints
from shrillness to a crashing bass –
Rachmaninoff jabbing his bruises –
A scholar is haunted by his opposite –
A Grand Inquisitor
An obese Prime Ministir –
A fellow clerk with good taste in neck ties,
his love is for schnapps and French liqueur,
like the cackle of boys from my tree-lined street
with their rugby boots and souped up cars,
their liqueur is sour, their laughter does not catch,
so he kisses the Inquisitor's bloodless lips,
he'd rather crack up than admit
there's nothing in this world
but what you can touch.

I'm mad – like the scholar –
a silent clerk brimming with satiric fury
at the dull neckties around him,
eyes shadowed in perpetual hangover,
always stepping aside
for a nincompoop soldier,
his sword clatters but he has no mind,
I laugh at him in a shock of sympathy,
my untidy thoughts thrash like the piano
then stop with a bang, I drop the book.

Silence.
The book face down on dusty carpet,
with crusts of mouldy pizza.
Why does it not somersault,
trailing multicoloured sparks?
I want to climb into its pages
a captive animal writhing in a bag
wrestling with a thrilling mind,
resisting a little – no I'm not that!
but slowly becoming a Karamazov.
I want to go to Russia
but it doesn't exist –
certainly not here.

I open the law books on my desk.
The words swim
I cannot understand them.
How will I get to the High Court?
On the last night of my life,
I want to spend thousands on a spree
with crates of champagne
peasant dancers playing tambourines,
or grotesque singers and drag-queens,
like Dimitry– to win a kiss
from who?
I cannot say.
I haven't met him yet.

I am not Dostoyevsky.
I am not Rachmaninoff.
I have no voice
but for a parody
of the last thing I read.
Is there not a world outside –
neon, shouting bars and crazy boys?
I do not know.
I've hardly been there.
Will I pick up the book?
Instead I open the door
and look…

Boarding House

A patio ringed with rusting iron,
a mosaic full of holes
dusty like a mothballed jigsaw.
A columned doorway
sheds multicoloured flakes of paint
down to grimy sandstone.
A crumbling mansion
worn lino inside
stained with booze, the smell of a urinal.
The filament of a naked bulb
flickers through the long dark corridor.
Door after door
edged with slivers of light,
the bruised monologues of daytime television,
a man spits 'Fuck' so heartfelt, a woman weeps.
Is this the end of the line?
Until I hear the storm of Beethoven's Pastoral,
and I know you're in there.

Cat

A dank room expands
in purple lamplight.
A cat yawns on your lap,
she purrs as you stroke her
rumpled black fur shudders to life.
I'm a tiny reflection in the brown pool of her eyes
and in the cold blue satire of yours.
She bares her claws and hisses.
'She's a stray, like me.
She hates professors, they want to dissect her.'
Beethoven's strings slither down to brooding.
I say nothing
I touch her matted fur.
She rolls as I scratch
her soft breathing belly.
You are stroking her torn ears,
she hums with the cellos.
'She likes you.' And at last you smile.
You are gentle
and for a moment
we merge in the cat's contentment.

You Draw Me

In silence
you fidget scowling
uncomfortable in your skin
like me
then your eyes shift
probing deeply into mine,
playing havoc with my shyness.
You pick up a pad
and draw me
bold curves in charcoal
your body now still,
all its life in your hands and stare.
Your charcoal quickens,
I see veins around your irises
redden with a playful light,
I'm drawn into your focus
I raise my head high
as you dot, shade,
deleting and restoring.
You take from me
transfer me to your pad
your fingers blackened,
time's nagging static slows
to a strange tranquillity,
only the charcoal leaps and scratches.

I do not like what I see.
One eye a gaping hollow
one a pool of muddy water in shadow
my lips tightly pursed.
You have changed me
no longer a coddled schoolboy
but an old/ young man
questioning his hurts.
'Why only one eye?'
'You're split,' you say
'You only half know yourself.'
I quiver with resentment.
I want you – but how?
I want to find a way
to distort the truth
to nettle you, to astonish you!
For a moment
I want to be you
or flee – and never see you again.

Endgame

You to play.
Beckett's face is staring
from a tattered volume of his games,
his mouth a twisted smile
like your body
lounging on a torn velvet couch
swathed in blackness
your slender fingers expressive
opening to invite me in
then closing in a fist
as the cat sprints in circles and yowls.
Portraits of women – and me –
wild like the cat with faraway eyes,
swirl with slashes of red and blue.
Everything is distorted here
like a precocious Picasso nightmare
shifting and searching for a shape.
The room is a cranium,
we train a telescope through the window
on the zero and grey outside,
we amputate slices
we float down a river
jostling with Rimbaud's ecstatic amoeba
feeding on snot and dark blue wine
as sirens and traffic and weeping
from neighbouring rooms seeps in.

What am I doing here?
Why do you want me here?
All the mess in my head,
the cacophony of voices
tearing me in pieces
starts to merge in my gestures,
my voice leaps with unlikely laughter,
you drain the cask's bladder
into our purple blotched cups,
we stroke the cat, feeling her scars,
we're speaking together
in a tangled rhythm.
Art starts here.

Nightclub

As I dive into the ocean,
arms flail in a purple flashing wave.
Brittle lyrics like washes of foam
hide the depths, the dark corners,
the sharks chasing fluorescent shoals.
She wants to kiss like an angel
(but how do angels kiss?)
Oh I'm in love, I'm in love, I'm in love
again and again, all meaning depletes,
a stamping on the platform above,
a beat like a hailstorm –
(are these your words or mine?)
The now people glow
there's only now, no past, no future,
no fear or anxiety.
(How we laugh about them together!)
I strut before a wanton ambling nymph –

(ha – no books here either, especially Shakespeare).
Just me – and all the others.
How to silence this static,
tying my body in knots,
as stiff as a lawyer
who's lost all control,
can my dance encircle
his beckoning body,
but he looks away
scorched by my glance,
heads swivel, looking up, looking down,
looking round and through me,
where is a needful ear to speak to,
but waves of musical love still crash,
turning my words to mime.
Rum burns, sliding down my oesophagus,
snorting fire through my nostrils with my smoke.

Boom

Today there's a tremor
bursting at your edges,
you parody my primness –
'How are you, captain?'
I don't want to play.
I tell you, 'I'm fine.'
'Loosen your strings
you're like a tin soldier,
did your parents forget
to wind you today?'
I stand and swear at you,
a boom in my voice
I've never heard before.
'I'm going,' but I stare
bursting at the edges like you.

'Touché!
I was a cornered animal too.
Hit back some more.'
I sit down,
the boom still echoes
a thrill in my eyes
a new shade in my voice,
then a bass riff splutters
with the spite of Nick Cave's song,
a spurt of wine in my cup.

Fathers

You to play.
We exchange fathers,
mine reading on a well worn couch
yours a judge in rugby boots,
head of a table of drunken lawyers
fluffing their gowns, boasting of marlin
dragged on hooks behind their boat,
trained tongues tear each other and the world.
Whereas mine
dives from his cushions
into a planet of robots
two-headed creatures and time machines.
He emerges from a misty jungle,
his eyes skim in and out,
for a moment the explorer
then the silent, tidy lounge room
until he sees me
wondering at him
waiting to ask him a question…

…like you, at the foot of the table
making elaborate paper gliders,
guffaws as they quaff good red.
They are stuffed, you are skinny
you stammer, you drop the ball,
your father takes your paper glider
and stomps on it – you're a disappointment
not a strapping Kiwi lad at all.

I giggle at your images
as you squirm within them…
as my father's stare sharpens –
why are you unhappy?
What – you like boys?
You have everything to look forward to
so many people are dying,
his stare aches with love
a frightened love
his eyes a pool falling inwards like mine,
naked boys gesture, a silent howl,
am I a disappointment too?
I now stare helplessly at you
I want to transform,
rewrite the world like you.

My father wryly smiles at yours.
They shake hands as we draw them,
your father warmly talks to mine
how they love a glass of fine red!
Yours is so witty
he could turn chambers gossip
into epigrams sharp enough
to slice Oscar Wilde! A raconteur too!
He scores the final try
as fifteen sweaty hands lift him high
covered in mud, rapturous cheers,
he motions to you, follow me
but you give him the finger
clutching a guitar.

My father kicks his feet up in New York bars
then a drive to California in a clapped-out car.
At sunset, he looks out over the Grand Canyon.
His voice chokes
as he tells your father the story,
his coils of emotion unwinding.

Then suddenly a thud –
a pile of thick reports
hem them both in an office
under cold strobe lights
dictating 'dear sir' over and over
like a cracked record
all their hilarity sucked down a plughole,
as a cluster of suits hustle for promotion.
They want to scream and dance
like madmen, so do we.
My father is still staring, silent.
Then he sees yours.
They click heals, shake hands with a bow,
tut tutting in turn about their wayward sons.
We are our fathers.
I want to rip up this draft of my life.

Maze

There are no words.
They stop here.
In the emptiness beyond them
are men and boys
circling and searching.
Keys jangle on their wrists
a dozen arms
reaching from the glow of twisting torsos,
faces with shadows for eyes
what terror!
A dark metallic beat
a clammy touch
an electric jolt.
I am repelled
I am awakened
no more words
no muddled thoughts,
I'm circling and searching.
I chase him
as he flees into darkness
his caress shakes my guts,
my body cries
to be touched again
to touch, to kiss.
My legs stride
through this maze
where every shadow promises
to end my aloneness.

He closes the door.
He knows what to do
do I?
My brain is cut away
floating astonished above me.
Breath swells his glistening chest
a delicious not quite smoothness
the taste of sweetened salt.
Red freckles float
beneath a down of hair
smeared with sweat flowing from his pores,
my body breathing with him,
I see my shapeliness
as he glances up and down me.
I writhe as he pushes me down
my needfulness shifting into him.
How I want his wanting,
the power of all of him.
My brain mutters 'you should not do this'
like someone else, not me,
it's me who shouts aloud
'Morrre!'
as he shrieks with laughter
a wave shatters through his body,
for a moment I am whole.

He brushes back my hair
so gentle
he is transparent like me.
A pause, then he shifts,
we're two awkward bodies again.
He blows me a kiss. 'See you later.'
The condom stayed on, didn't it?
I pick up my sodden towel
from the slippery vinyl bench.
I'm muddled again.

The street unravels

Furious boys cling in a pack.
Out of their depth,
do they come from a street like mine?
They search for men like me to annihilate
annihilate themselves, the terror of choice,
upending garbage, a windscreen shatters with their spite.
Do they see the kisses under my shirt,
my hair glistens wet
on a dry summer night,
what happened to that condom?
Where is he?
He could be one of them,
were his eyes dark
or shining with veins of demonic yellow light?
Was he my lover – or my murderer?
I want to kick a wall
rampage with the boys
their shouts catch in my throat.
A laughing boy with green hair
touches another's hand, nails painted black.
Please let them kiss – love is the only antidote,
they walk together, absorbed.
A line of brightly coloured drunks
jostle, flecked with neon
preening themselves at a door,
others spill out, one is ejected
writhing flat on his face on the pavement.

I'm depleted
floating above my body,
my thoughts waiting in ambush
to cross examine me like the barrister I should be –
he pokes at my chest, he scowls
then he strips off his gown
and becomes a shapely shadow.
He motions me at the door of the cubicle, we kiss,
a purple mark on my neck – he was real –
as the boy with green hair waves.
They fade, leaving only…
streetlights glowing blue
with flickers of ruby and emerald.
I'm walking away…
to nod in an armchair, safe
as I read Shakespeare's bloody revenges
my toes in plush carpet
as mother and father coo and fuss?
No – that image is flat,
it's torn apart by your voice
rollicking and twisting
like the lines on your portraits.
Your haunted house is close.
Will the light be on?

Bonfire of Barristers

Together we light a bonfire of barristers,
flaming trolleys of leather-bound judges.
The summer clerk moons at his mentor
his wig falls off as he chases me,
I turn to him and poke out my tongue.
Politicians with crinkle-cut hairdos
hoover up money
followed by a gaggle
of purple-haired vamps
in steel-capped boots and feathers
with shave foam on their faces,
cat o' nine tails in their dainty hands.
Did I say that or you?
We turn into fleas
on the set of a soap opera,
actor and actress forget their lines
as we spring around and bite them
gorgeous in our deformity,
leaving welts on their flawless skin
as the barbecue explodes.
My voice bounces with your hilarity.
My story grows, it amplifies
I find it in you,
my vagabond, *my foul bunch-backed toad,*
you turn it all around
into the grimmest of fairy tales,
a stupid boy lost in a thorny forest
fuel to the wildness of our laughter.

Another Walk

I walk along a sandstone wall.
A junky nods in delight
quivering lashes on empty eyes,
his body opens to the sky
cold and bluish like a waxwork.
Euphoria – I want that – or is it death?
A jagged line of boys – so young! –
offer themselves with a sneer
to all those (like me) who cast a sidelong glance
cars slow, a door slams,
they laugh in a jaded camaraderie
cheeks glowing in bright tank tops.
But just across the road,
behind bland orange brick
boys and men wither
to yellow skin on bones,
yesterday vigorous, searching like me,
with the courage to be wild.
The reaper with his scythe
holding a shrivelled skull
leaps at me from my television.
What happened to that condom?
I'm the best, the dux,
awaiting a life of endless achievement
but that's my old cardboard cutout.
Now I have flesh, my blood is surging.

It cannot be now!
In the circling and searching of my thoughts,
the venom of my self-reproach,
can I find the power to leap?
I want to mix these images
into an intoxicating brew.
The only one who understands is you.

You tell me
'You are so alive
You walk between two worlds
a fearsome passageway
these demons are kindly ones
sent to try you,
maybe I'm one of them.'

My Clown

My mouth moves
I cannot speak.
There's no longer a threat
in the blue of your eyes
bruised with mascara,
I'm dizzy in the spiral of your irises.
You are so gentle
as you read in me
all your deep lacerations
twisting into new creations,
you've been there
riding on inner chaos like mine!
I'm between two strong horses
pulling in opposite directions –
you too – that's why we search!
A smile now breaks on your reddened lips
shifting onto mine.
You get me
You're showing me the way.

You are my clown.
I smear lipstick on my mouth
I shadow my eyes with purple,
my body relaxes
lounging on the couch.
All the broken pieces
are gathering into a story.

I nestle my head in your chest.
You shake your head.
'Don't spoil things.
I'm not in your life for that.'
'Well then – for what?'
You laugh, pouring me a drink.

Trickster Spirit

We're trickster spirits,
ready to leap
with a cat's agility
purring laughter
baring our teeth with a hiss.
We sit on a grassy island
with a single palm tree, watching.
My third eye pierces under skin,
the swaggerers dragging a cartload of fear
wild transformation behind gloomy eyes.
Greyness falls
shifting into green, then blue, then sickly green,
the outlines of bodies are blurring.
A punk boy slithers,
sheathed in blackness
etched with tattoos, flashes of metal,
ready to strike with poison fangs.
That drunk is in pieces –
face like a broken statue
covered with moss
a duckbill,
he crawls on webbed feet,
where does he belong?
A angel shakes their stripy tail
of pink and orange feathers,
will you wrap me in your wings?
Can I climb into your costume?

A soprano warbles
as a filthy spotted dog howls
he can't strum the guitar with his paws
but coins clink into his bowl.
Ducks quack, wobbling away
from a herd of bison on a buck's night.
Demented shiny pills speed by
screeching on red, revving on green
fouling the air with their excretions.
We sit on the island
running a commentary –
will this zoo
turn and devour each other,
is it a nature documentary or football?
Our voices are suave, very BBC.
We're here to bewilder you – and ourselves.
Here to jumpstart the heart of this city –
or is the city jumpstarting us?
Will we join?
Or are we trapped in a box?

Performance

The smite of your hammers
the ringing of bells
then you appear,
as Beethoven plays,
tying himself in knots.
'It's done.'
Hands shaking, you wriggle it free.
'Can you read it to me?'
Your body electric with mental gymnastics,
you jolt me to my feet.
As I read
my body unravels
from music, poetry, self-reproach
my endless unfocused lust,
my belly splutters and gags,
my voice deepens and rises…

I'm buoyed by the greasepaint,
a red light snaps above me
my body shifts open.
My eyes stand out
like black olives dripped
in glistening oil,
I've never seen such seductive olives.
The audience quiver
twisting with awkward laughter,
as I throw acid in the faces
of squadrons of marauding businessmen,
sucking the living marrow
from everything, including me.

I refashion clichés as weapons,
blowing the whistle on the cat in the bag
until they hang me,
kicking the chair from beneath
as they adore my erection,
to gasping titters and hysterics,
the illusion draining as I bow.
You shake my hand,
My black eyes an exaggeration of yours
the green at their centre gushing outwards
my red lipstick a death in life.
In the dressing room
I wash off the clown
hang up his billowing cape
pensive and clumsy again
but with something of you still in me.
I hug my fellow actors
as they wipe their faces clean,
the world has shifted a little.
Later, alone in a bar's thumping loveless music,
I glimpse a beautiful man
slipping away in a mime of laughter.

Angel

A park by the harbour.
It's midnight.
A breeze chills my skin
through gaps in my coat.
I want to go home,
but somehow you shepherd
the fragments of my yawning senses.
The sky is grey.
The clouds drift.
You want to take me over.
The water flickers with lights on the other shore.

Your head is tilted to the sky.
Your ribs expand and fill.
I'm no longer beside you.
I'm there within your deepening breaths,
my head hinges upwards like yours,
as the clouds glide
unstoppable,
faint puffs sharpen
into vast headless birds.
Trails of feathers spin,
unravelling into spider thread
and swallowed
by a slash of nothingness.
A low hum of music,
as you whisper, 'Angel!'

Eyes widen and squint
with dirty cotton lashes,
no iris, just a gaping hole
tinged with the city's purple light.

'Just clouds at night, just clouds at night.'
No – they're something more.
I'm shaking like you.
Tears are running down
the stillness of your cheeks,
you're panting with astonishment,
I'm afraid for you, afraid for me
I shake myself awake, until…

…above our heads a branch,
circling leaves glint silver
as the moon winks
through gaps in the clouds,
a blinded eye
bruised with rust
with thin infected capillaries.
So ancient
for a moment defiant
then slowly muffled
by the glowing, monstrous clouds.
'Rapture,' you whisper.

I break right away.
I look you up and down.
Your head is stretching from your body
like a string is tugging you upwards.
Angels?
You're mad.
The park drains to trees,
grey light on the harbour,
clouds blown by freezing wind.
You want to swamp me
until there's nothing left of me.
You're driving me mad.
I see red brick of apartment blocks
a cackle of boys sculling beers,
all the lights going out
in windows across the shore.
This city is so bland.
I look back up again
to find what you see,
searching for your breath's rhythm,
as your trance slowly breaks.
Your smile is radiant.
You've won again.

Schooner

We sparkle in a rush of free association,
sitting in a mess of bottles
as Morison and Ludwig trade punches.
Each gulp of a schooner of wine
thickens a film on your bulging eyes.
It runs through you like a panic
stinging your brain
your arms chopping down
demolishing the air around you
spittle sprays
from the messy purple of your lips,
now torn downwards in a scowl.

I speak.
You do not hear.
You're beating on a pane of glass
that hems you in
with voices refracting and echoing
your father, toxic critics, bloated politicians,
please!
I've heard all this before,
let's cast them all loose with our grinning irony,
and wander so eclectic through the gorgeous books
spattered with booze on the floor.
You unhinge yourself
with every poisonous sip,
an actor whose only lines
are a bitter tirade,
you stick to the script
as the theatre burns around you,
the audience have gone.
Except for me…

You sweep me away,
like I'm just one of a swarm of bees
swooping to attack you.
You're now hoarse
trumpeting your greatness
a puppet in a dirty punk suit top,
you stagger, you rise
as if pulled up by hidden strings,
so broken, so fragile –
What can I do without you?
I'm still transfixed.

You shake
sensing my hostility in your gut,
all empathy cut away
from the fineness of your mind.
You magnify the fears
I've quietly confided to you
into monsters,
you're the one who can save me,
I plummet into smallness
but as I crash,
I bounce back up.

I take you by the shoulder
shouting STOP!
into the murky panic of your eyes.
You push me away,
I topple.
You take the schooner glass
smash it on the table
spattering me with drops of wine,
it's now a jagged circle of knives.
I face you
in my own drunken swagger,
'You won't. You can't.'
You drop it,
a sudden flicker of warmth in your eye.
I flee.

Focus

Thoughts circle in yellow
falling from trees.
Streetlights shed blue,
flickers of ruby and emerald.
Traffic limps then zooms.
I hear the slap of my footsteps
I jump over a puddle,
spilled chips oozing with mud.
I hug my body,
not dressed for chilly wind.
The street is in sharp focus, snoozing.

I do not wobble.
Everything intoxicating
has drained from my brain.
I wipe all makeup from my face.
My limbs are loosening
from the rush of adrenalin.
I'm watching, still watching, listening
to the rhythm of my footsteps, only mine.
I'm alone.

The bars pulse with needfulness.
They want me, they want my body.
I scuttle past the grassy island
I'll never sit there again.
Everyone who passes
cannot hide a teasing quirk
a pleasing asymmetry,
they sigh, they cough,
shuffling, running, stopping still
everyone is incomplete – like me.

The muscles in my legs
swell and tighten as I walk,
my forearms have a light down of hair
my buttocks are firm
my breath inflates my guts.
How glad I am to be separate.
I do not want to lose myself
in knotting bodies,
in some twisted, spiteful mind
in a poem's maze of qualifications.
No I just want to be next to a man
pulsing with warmth, clenched with an awkwardness –
'How was your day? How was work?
What music do you like?'
and not care about the answers
as I watch his breathing chest,
the shyness of eyes raising to mine.

I'm breathing beside him
it's clumsy, it's sweaty
we apologise, we laugh
we stop, change position,
working out what we want to do.
There's now a pause
seemingly endless,
my face is twisting,
a panting in my body
then streams of tears.
His arms are around me.
'What's the matter?'
'I've lost a friend.'
But now a man is next to me.

The Captain

A man is staring
he looks like my father
but he's not
he's awkward like me
in the rush of searching bodies.
We look back from the grassy island.
I'm shaking.

He freezes when he sees you
his mouth gapes, he wants to speak
but the distance is too great.
He takes a notebook from his pocket and
writes, stares, writes.
He doesn't belong, his clothes cut from another time,
jaded revellers pass through his body
a middle-aged man leering
his smile so gentle and knowing.
I want to ask him a question
find out who he is
but I already know
I leap up but you stop me.

'That's the Captain,' you chuckle
'writing and rewriting a novel
no one will ever read
but you and me.
He's never heard of Spontaneity.
He reports for duty at his desk
at exactly the same time every day.

The sharpness of his crystalline phrases
slowly blur to manure.
He stares in the mirror
waiting for a blinding flash,
his plump cheeks droop.
He's looking for inspiration –
in us.'

An agitated lunatic stamps
as if he could topple all the towers in the city,
dead blue eyes varnished to his face,
his outline quivers and jumps – like yours.
He heckles the Captain
just as you heckle me.
You write in your notebook
your next play is forming
our painful banter will be staged.
I'll act out my demon.
I smile.
One day I'll be a writer.

2

The palm tree is gone
from the grassy island.
It's quiet now, almost orderly.
Still the urgent seeking for a mate,
but young eyes are clear
not veering away from the straight ahead,
no swivelling heads searching for a shape
they only look for what you can touch.

Except for two side by side.
A gentle boy full of adoration
the other sneers from purple lips
his body quivers with disenchantment
their gestures like mirrors
voices jostle and rise
as they nettle each other
to find a single vision of what they see.
The younger sighs, he's me
so easy to hurt so lovely, he doesn't know it.
I'm writing in my notebook.
I rise from beside him
to face myself
I cannot warn me
we're so entwined…
Victor opens his lips to speak
he rolls his eyes at what I've become
and smiles with warm complicity
as a madman proclaims the end of the world.

I'm the Captain
writing and rewriting.
Caution yearning to tear off its clothes
two sides of my brain
chattering over a bottle of red
the wrecking ball of your voice
leaps with an upward inflection
I pick up my pen and write.

Angel of Death

You drink from a long neck
on the balcony of a tower block
through rotting teeth,
our banter wide awake as you slur,
trailing off as we remember…
You turned yourself inside out,
screaming your abuse
as passers by scuttled and snickered.
You're safe now
hiding out bewildered,
the laceration of your irony,
directed outward and inward
has quietened.
They can't give you a belting,
kick you into a paddy wagon,
the Angel of Death
shaking and so vulnerable
beyond help.
He flickers in your eyes
as you drink,
you can still see right through me.
'Why don't you write again?'
You snort.
'Why don't you stop?'
I shrug as your images
take shape at the edge of our gossip,
a sudden moment of laughter.

I'm poised in my study.
Your plays sit in a folder,
a few played to scattered houses.
The city quickly drowned them out.
You fell silent
unable to ridicule
the mediocre echo of social chatter.
I want you to rise again in me,
a clown in greasepaint
strong enough to laugh
in the white heat of regimented anarchy,
turning the elements to beauty.

Victoria Street
A Kings Cross Fantasia 1973

Helen – a brightly dressed, dissatisfied woman, 50s
Vanessa – a showgirl, 20
Louise – an intellectual woman fleeing the suburbs, 30
Michael – a young gay poet, 21
Tony – a bouncer at various Kings Cross Hotels, 30

I: Helen

Hello, I'm Helen, a friend of Juanita Neilsen, back from Victoria Street Kings Cross in 1974, and this is my terrace. Come in, Come in…

Rust pockmarks on wrought iron,
a coat of arms
repeating and repeating
its black paint flaking
royal blue of walls and ceilings peeling
like my make-up
that cannot smooth the furrows on my face.
I pour a rotten glass of wine.

On the next balcony, men remake the world.
Their talk will bring the system crashing down.
Karl Marx, his white beard stained with booze;
a book with pages flapping in the wind
eggs them on, until they forget him
and talk of some flirtatious woman
(not me!) they want and cannot get.
Oh men and their endless bravado
and nothing ever changes,
I prefer to look a branch with fresh leaves
swaying over the balcony,
wild spray of green glowing in the sun
a play of life, light and shadow
mixing with my smoke, the sharp tang of red
so much more interesting than…

How anxious I feel!
This house is a haven, a paradise
after all my years of wandering
'Victoria Street, my Home!'
I shout to the carousing revolutionaries
'They'll throw us on the street!
Get ready for the fight.'
They tell me, 'It's cool – she'll be right,'
and more of such crushing banality,
the yawning mantra of this country.
Oh I love them all dearly
my maverick neighbours and friends,
but I cannot join them now…

This terrace teeters on a cliff.
At the back you can see the city's heart.
Office boxes piling higher
spreading wider
with giant letters shouting
DALGETY GOLDFIELDS AMP
BANK OF NEW SOUTH WALES drooling spittle
playthings of some spoilt child.
I close my velvet curtains
but it changes nothing
the boxes multiply, they want to leap the valley
tearing down trees to make wads of banknotes,
sneering businessmen hold hands with thugs
the concrete towers spring up around them.

City workers in their own little boxes
clicking their tongues at the nightly news
oh the views are divine! the blue of the harbour!
new house of sails where fat ladies shriek,
too good here for commies, loafers, degenerates…

The young in each others arms
pour in from the snoozing suburbs
the world changes
with every kiss, each strum of their guitar.
They demand – don't take our bodies
with all their joy and playfulness
to smash in your filthy war!
I want them, these dissatisfied ones!
Only they can stop
the men in suits making notes on clipboards,
the goons closing in, some cash if you leave.
My house is almost empty, two friends have left.
I'm alone.

Louise in the Suburbs

I cook by rote
the meat is dry
our eyes drained of colour
like the vegies, all flavour gone.

His red wine nauseates
his sentences finish in my head
the moment his grumbling starts
an endless chewing of gristle
an echo of his dried up friends
as he trails off and stares.
I've forgotten how to love
I know the clammy coldness
of his next touch and his next,
he's drained to a tiresome shadow of himself.
I wanted to gather some fiery collage
from books dead on the shelf behind him
our thoughts stepping in crescendo
towards some astonishing newness.
Now I only mutter as I ask to leave the table
to sit in the chilly darkness of our bedroom
encircled by his brooding, and he in mine.

It ended in a mirror.
Trickling blood warms my cheek
eye shadowed with a puff of pinkness
taking on a purple hue
red quickening streams of tears.
It was only then I felt the pain
my eye pressed deep in its socket
against my panicking brain.

A drop congeals on Dickens' beard,
the scholar I saw in him
now the empty motion of his punches.
I'm standing tall
quivering in the mirror
it is over.
I'll take one bag
I have no friends but his
for them I'm his younger, graceful copy.
I want a space to see my thoughts
take on a clarity of passion
like my battered face.
I am afraid he will return
wheedling, crushing me with smallness.
There's only my parents, too like him.
Or a café in Kings Cross.

Michael in the Suburbs

It's no longer my room
it belongs to my double.
For years he slept in my body.
He absently walked the tree lined avenue.
The worlds he explored were always far away
a voyeur of ancient tragedy
of obsolete maps and family trees.
I always knew it was not enough.
My sister and parents are sleeping
but I can not.

I take off my greasy waiter's shirt –
what would Rashkalnikov think?
I lie on my childhood bed
eiderdown blue, embroidered with cars.
I fling it away
squirming in gorgeous nakedness.
Beyond the billowing curtains
are rows of dark houses, secretly dreaming.
This a home for him, but not for me
as his law books reproach me on the shelf
and my body explodes with caresses
it can never find here.
I reach for the cassette and stare into
the shine of humorous eyes,
the wild mop of curls on the wall.
The answer is…

Michael on Darlinghurst Road

I move through ever changing light
as jumping pig and pussycat
cast an alluring red
tinged with green
over clusters of searching faces
but I cannot settle on anyone
as shoes jostle, swerving on asphalt.
A seagull squawks at chips in the gutter.
Love songs intertwine
from each new door
in blue and purple balls of light
glowing in the bubble of schooners.

Drinkers pulsate, gesturing and dancing.
Faces jump out from the rev of cars honking.

I'm here for myself
not trapped in a tightening, unloving knot of men
with clenched arms and ogling faces.
The checks in the starch of my shirt
are circling, jumping
so far away from my room's dull truth
of static white light.
I'm revolted, I'm electric
I want to run home
but I open my arms
and let it all shake me,
as a handsome drunk
knocks me off my feet
and smiles as he scuttles away.
I look up from dodging boots and stilettos.
Tree leaves flutter with pinkness
as the cat's purple tongue licks its green whiskers.
It stretches and jumps, then gives me a wink.
I'm here, I'm alone
as love twists high in guitar and song
boy fights with girl as engines screech.
I'm alone with all this
not the reproach of dark voices
and my eiderdown in baby blue
embroidered with cars.

A Lost Elf: Helen

(walking on Darlinghurst Road)

Their loveless strutting,
stubbled bullies in suits
fat fingers making fists
no flowing gestures or caresses
but they look round and through me,
their roving hands seek softer targets,
men and their desire for a quick explosion.
I'm invisible at last, and empty
do I miss their leering smiles
pulling beers for thousands of men, hundreds of bars?
The ghost of a gorgeous lustful stare
flickers in my brain
an unbuckling belt, rushed words of love
his captivating face, what story did he tell?
My favourite scarf is faded and frayed,
does satin glow on a tired body
treasures found one night in Soho
just the baubles of an ageing whore.
My endless seeking is all that's left…

…a lost elf
in a dress stained with dirt
the fabric translucent, a hint of slender beauty,
looking inward, spiralling downwards like me
a bruise on a cheek scarred with pimples
so easy to hurt, tumbling over the edge…

Vanessa

Scarlet lips curl in a smile
neon brightens her shadowed eyes
a dress in black satin you never see where I come from –
I touch her scarf, her flowing hair.
She takes it off
spangled and fragrant with wildflower brooches…
and with a whoosh, it's around my head
I spin and she laughs
then I stop and stare at her again
trying to stand with a bit of her grand – what is it?
I take her cigarette, and smoke with her easy flourish,
she touches the bruise on my cheek
so gently I want to cry…
A freakish soul to laugh with?

Vanessa in the Suburbs

We roved bare-chested
reeking with sweat
half starved muscles
ready to strike.
We gave our finger to the world
raucous like scraping metal,
her photo singing in my pocket.

I mirrored their swagger
the bored scowl
exploding to a jerky flurry
of shit mixed with words
at the stuffed shirts, the purple perms in lace
the houses peeling in ramshackle rows.
I master then sharpen
their whistles and grunts
to ever bigger talk, a new bravado.
They follow me, I follow them
but then, like it's on a better planet
a green silken dress
flaps on a clothes line,
they don't see it,
but do they see my blush?
My shout is the loudest
at naked flesh
torn from a magazine
in their shaking hands,
she's smiling just for me
my lips smile back.
I bask in their arousal.
My defences are fraying
I raise my fists
spoiling for a fight.

2

'He hangs there like a spider.
Let's crush him.'
He stays too long
like he's glued to the urinal,
he winked at me once
I winked back
but now
we hold him
smash his head on porcelain
blood drips into piss
he flails
stick limbs, ugly face
like a grasshopper
until he flops, crushed in our grasp.
Defiance pulses from his irises
questioning just me
something passes between us.
I kick him and leave.
I vomit outside
a moment alone
to plot how to steal
the silken green dress.

3

I take her photo from my pocket.
I place it on the mattress.
I tear off my tank top and shorts.
She's wrapped in velvet
shining curls fall
over her naked shoulders,
the poise of her crimson lips
about to burst into song.
I want to merge into her
but I can't,
my body in tangles.
I touch the green dress.
The boys crudely call to me like demons
as I stand
searching for her shapely flow.
Nothing. I'm nothing
I'm a void in between them.
I want to die.
I cut my chest with a knife.
I bleed in pain. I'm alive.
I can't die now and always be
this spotty empty boy.
I take a bag
pack the green dress
her photograph and the torn centrefold.
I'll miss the boys and they'll miss me.
My first loves, I grew with them.

Helen

Twenty-five years ago
like you
I ran
Whispers were all around me
I wanted to laugh with men in bars
but I felt their contempt
no kisses in a back lane
as hands tear my clothes and they're gone.
I ran to find a place where…
a generous place, a refuge, but…
but they found me
and gagged my accusations
as God's avengers.
They put me in the mad house
with other quietly furious women
or howling like me…

Alone on the street
searching for fantasy
then the glint of diamonds
sharp across my face.
'I have a job, a bit of adventure
for a feisty girl like you.'

Her name was Tilly Devine.
Her slashing tongue barked
orders to men in dishevelled suits,
her scowl wrapped in a silken scarf.

A room with velvet cushions, girls swagger
with brittle poise sniffing Charlie.
Drunks tear me open and boast,
or cower abject on my breast
again and again, six times a night.
I'd collapse in exhaustion.

How I wanted her strength in fury
more brutal than her thugs
my lips fixed in a sneer like hers,
no longer a frightened girl
rehearsing fake laughter.

A new girl cries so I caress her.
I sense my hidden flow of kindness.
I didn't want to shrivel with curses!
I fled to protect a something I couldn't name.

'I have a house, a crumbling mansion
in a lively tree-lined street.
And a room full of dresses…'

Vanessa

Up the rickety darkened stairs
then we walk into a cave
smelling of joints and wilting flowers.
She lights candles streaming with flaking wax.
The room reveals its treasures
dress racks coated with a sheen of dust
her red lips smile over yellowing teeth.

My fingertips glide over satin
glowing lame, the rough warmth of tweed
a needle drops on a walnut phonogram.
A yearning song shivers through my body
I open my arms
my breathing deepens
my mouth begins to move
fabrics tremble, pitch-black, blue of oceans
taunting scarlet, orange of egg yolks,
I touch, I want them
to blossom on my body.
She laughs
with a tinge of phlegm and sorrow
and I laugh too
it's a fairy tale all around me
the story of a strong woman.

Helen

One feather, five, then twenty
she runs their softness across her face.
I comb her long unruly hair
as she twists and dances
breathing shiraz and a smoky lovesong.

I take to a silken dress with my scissors
glossy with forgotten flirtation,
an admirer smiling as he kissed me
when I wore it long ago.
We work together talking
needle and thread weaving with our stories…

Vanessa's Story: Car Job

I shiver under the streetlight
just to show some enticing flesh
bitten by the winter breeze
dreaming of pavlova with strawberries and cream.
Others preen at the edge of shadow,
our craving clusters us
drives us apart
vying to be seen,
our acid gossip quickly shifts
to nail flailing fury
if you cross the line.
We wait for a car
tensely jostling for space
against a sandstone wall
which if you stop to listen
still rattles with the breath
of prisoners fighting and flirting there before us,
a gathering of the thwarted.

A car slows
shaking with anticipation,
a plume of warm exhaust.
I stand nonchalant
I tingle with his scrutiny
a shadowy telepathy of wanting
I know he's picked me.

Does a fumble at the door latch
break the spell I'm casting?
Squeaking vinyl as he shifts
my foot rests on a smiling doll
I touch a quivering hand
as his body twists,
with a caress, I slap him away.
A crumpled note, I ask for triple
I glisten in his pleading eyes,
the doll's face squawks a laugh.
I'm his lost youth, his freedom.
Springing from a cage in the suburbs,
a whipped little man asserts himself
ripping at my dress, touching flesh
it must be now, an unlit side street
then he unzips, reaching for my head.

My shaking hands contort behind me
searching for the eyelets on my blouse
so I can return to my silken composure
floating high above, milking men's lust.
I light a cigarette,
on the periphery, the others smirk –
I cannot ask their help.
My broken bloody body
will soon rest in some dumpster.

I'm a lost boy, dishevelled
looking for gentle hands to help
a freakish soul to laugh with
at my trick's feeble grunt
then his rage
as he pushed me from the car
cursing clawing for his cash,
my heart still thumping
he bruised me as I punched him
my beauty no protection
but I find a little calm
reaching for my lipstick…

There are colourful lights
glowing at the end of the street.
I walk from the cackle of hanged men,
towards a new chaos of possibility
the wild flirtation of cafés and bars
I play with the notes
and there's more if I stand again.
Oh never again!
I can dance
or bewitch my admirers with my idle thoughts.
And yet…I'm addicted
to the rush of adrenalin images.

Helen's Story: Soho

In London's cloudy damp,
I was freed from home's benumbing sunshine,
the colour was in flowing shawls,
comfortable with room to move
no more constricting formality
gyrating legs in minis
with a corseted blouse as a cheeky throwback,
I always played, putting unlike things together
to find a startling hilarity, the rule book was gone,
the past a whimsical palette to choose from.
A rough look with a silken glow
youthful flesh with a layer of glitter
as music blared electric
from overflowing bars.
Young men with luxuriant hair
sang to free the raucousness of love.
But just a few streets from Carnaby
the three piece suit, the rolled up umbrella
suspicious sideways glances.

Why did I return?
I had changed from a flapper to spinster
typing spiteful letters of demand.
All my spontaneity shrivelled,
again the madhouse beckoned.
Until I heard…
a little of my searching anger…
what I see and love in you…

voices of the dissatisfied
rising in excitement
searching out the new!
I found my crumbling mansion.

Strength in Beauty

We stitch on purple ruffles
a glow of diamantes,
fishnets from my Tilly days,
earrings from a Paris weekend,
a pillage of my life,
play of fabrics sampled and discarded,
open scissors, spools of thread.

Boy, feathers, lame, lipstick –
so much more than the sum of these parts
a strength in beauty I've always searched for,
I find it in her…

'You're ready!'
'For what?'
'Talent night at the Purple Onion.'
She snorts.
'For Les Girls. That's where I want to dance.'
She kisses my cheeks, then my lips.
I blush and pull away.
My love is in her joyous stance
and not in any kiss.
'And now, take me out. Dawn's my time.'

II: Tony and Vanessa

Tony and the Boss at the Venus Room

The Venus is jumping,
the girls all legs in minis
trays of glowing amber with ice
low light from a chandelier
shadows of men stumble with bravado.
The boss arrives
sitting at his centre table
the potency
of his jovial stare
tears inhibitions, notes fly from wallets
the revelry intensifies
animal shouts over jazz band jive.

Knowing he is watching,
I circle and smile
adjusting the buttons of my scarlet suit
flaunting its muscular line.
I keep the moment electric
spiralling not quite out of control
with a wink, a handshake, a threat
ready for a flying fist, a broken-off glass,
as girls hustle men to softly furnished rooms.

He beckons.
He wants me.
I sit, his eyes opaque stare playfully into mine.
'His dirty fingers in the till…'
He pauses as a waitress giggles
bringing us whiskies and ice…

'You know what to do.'
The quiet insinuation in his voice
cuts through the bellowing music
as the bar revolves around him
sweeping in cops who jump when he says,
he sits easy
fury wrapped in his well cut suit
easing into a chuckle as he jokes
a Walther bulges from his coat
he's ready to pounce at any intruder,
he came from nothing like me.
Now the Premier invites him to lunch.
'Yes boss.'
He trusts me.
I leave with a skip
shaking with a dread that makes me stronger.

Vanessa's Love Song

1

Naked in silence
I caress
the slash of a scar
poking from your chest hair,
rough pinkness like stitching
expands with your ribs as you snore.
There's only my body now and yours
still sweating on your rumpled sheets.

I'm dizzy in the vodka's bitter reek
as the cut knuckles of your hand
gently rest on my breast.
I kiss your imperfections.

2

The city is ours
framed in your window.
Shadowy buildings
with pinpricks of light
ride on the black
of the harbour's ink
thickening like treacle.

I start to sink.
You are writhing
coloured figments jostle
on your sleeping lids,
your scar is tearing
weeping blood and pus
or is it mine?

Rocking in the grey hush above us,
I see a frightened boy –
is it you? No, it's me –
hanging dresses touch his body.
He's hiding in a wardrobe
from…

Spittle from a mouth wide open,
a drunk is roaring
he's lurching and flailing
the slits of his eyes shed tears.
A shaking form searches for a shape –
is it yours or mine?

You unwrap yourself
clenching your fists
fragile lines of a half starved body
now curving with muscles,
you grasp his pleading throat.
The fabric of your suit is bursting as

I add another feather
a red damask shawl
a purple line to heighten
the staring blue of my eyes.
This is me now, this is you.
We dance as he multiplies
around us, whistling and cheering.

You awake with a wink
and wrap your arms around me.

3

Our drinks glow blue.
I touch the finely layered weave
of your unbuttoned suit.
A trumpet from the jazz band
sprints invisible steps to triumph.

We're at the centre
all around us ties are loosened
ropes of pearls and jiving shoulders
lover chases lover, glancing at me and you.
Before you came to the Cross,
you could only dream of this.
Now you're a manager here.
You have a Ford – a streamline – outside,
how it bellows and roars!
You tell me – not so long ago,
you stole them – I did too!
Notes stuff your wallet.
A gorgeous dress adorns me.
I leap to my feet, spinning wildly.
We chart their illicit journeys.

4

With delicate hands
you unbutton your shirt
coyly offering your body's power,
years of punching the bag
now awkwardly imploring,
you swivel your hips like a shy girl.

Your clumsy fingers grab at my skirt
I slap them away.
You wait
not daring to move.
I taunt you, unpeeling to
my skin's waxen glow.

Pert breasts like a tomboy,
I shake as I dare
my magician's finale
playing with your dread
your anticipation.
There it is, larger than yours
you're transfixed.
I push you to the wall and kiss you
the roughness of your stubble
tickles my bosom with giggles.
I'm a match for you, my love –
who's more of the outlaw?
Unchained now, we wrestle.
I pin you to the floor,
you sigh as you stare
and slowly I bend
and kiss your gasping lips.

Tony's Grace

We know he's home.
We know he's ready.
He's on the skids
booze, hammer and floozies,
he's pissed it away.
He jumps at us
swinging a baseball bat,
it bounces, singes my hair.

I lunge under
crack of rib under fist
a television crashes,
spewing its wiry guts.
My mate says enough
I cannot stop bloody fists.
My mate says enough.
I leap up whole.
He's broken
gargling blood in his throat.
A surge of adrenalin
A warm flood of grace.

Vanessa and Shirley at Les Girls

I cannot meet the mirror
I'm empty like the dresses
hanging on the rack.
Shirley
can I leap with you
soaring and plummeting on a gust
way over the orchestra,
notes spurting like blood from my throat
an exquisite sauce,
I sigh
a lump of purple glaring on my neck
it stings as I tease it
with a viscous blob of make-up
his kisses seem last year, not last night.

I touch the itch of gilded twill
silk as glossy as lips,
Helen stitched
her foot on the treadle
sequins glow
over red and purple lace,
her laughter resounds
a ridicule of dullness
then the venom of her stare,
'Let's find more strength than them.'
I chuckle as I gag.
The dancers are dressing,
fabric in strands like petals
starts to blossom on their bodies.
I embolden my make-up
the ghost of crazy Ophelia
throwing punches at the court,
we're freed from all constraint.
I'm nervous like a fever.

The stages shakes under our feet
as men quaff cocktails
pinching their wives,
they share our longing
for the world to be upended
just here, just now,
we turn the tables
on the men who've monstered us
the leering tables of bucks
burn with our acid beauty.

We curtsy to their cheers.
This is my life.

Tony Watches Vanessa

She stands out from the line
on legs like a sprinter
her body is hard
wrapped in soft fabric.
She chokes all the titters
gasps turn to whistles.
She's the bad girl
itching for a fight
wild until she changes
eating from your hand.

She's my twin, but stronger.
They all shake when I walk in
but I'm shaking now.
I don't want some giggling yes girl
I could be smashed tomorrow.
Vanessa unwinds me
she whispers fire in my ear.

The boss smiles like a shark.
He made this place.
He wrangles the rebels – like her, like me.
He'd rather make you laugh than kill you.
He's the master of mayhem.
He's the man.

He whispers, 'She's good, your girl
but she thinks too much.
There's ratholes in Victoria Street,
I want them cleaned out
they're stuffing a mate around.'
'Yes boss.'
A drunk is throwing punches.
I stride over and drop him
my knee busts his gut.

III: Michael

Michael on Darlinghurst Road
Reflections in Rhinestone

Waistcoats hand in hand with frocks
sailors lurching arm in arm
they all rush by
as I pause, a moment to breathe.

Only then do I see
laughter in rolling eyes
flowing beard in tangles,
his cape a dirty blanket
coins in a hat at blistered feet.

He sits on a bank's granite steps,
our faces reflect on rails of polished brass.
I reach into my pocket
but he shakes his grey head,
he welcomes me as I sit by him.

He wears a rhinestone necklace
balls of sparkling prisms
flashing in an aura of red and blue.
'We spin off our axis
we crash and we burn.'

A foreign accent – a knowing
rhythm from Europe's darkness.
Mocking men, blue-eyed in a pack
kick at his cap of coins
scattering, clattering on black,
they spin then they fall…

…I'm in a sunny playground,
they knock me to the ground and kick me
bloody lips shocked to numbness
my head smashing on asphalt…

…I like his blanket's pungency
as I lean into its warmth.
He touches my cheek, ruffles my hair,
my throat burns as I sip from his bottle.

He gives me a rhinestone
and in its multifaceted reflection,
my face shifts bewildered into gorgeousness.
'It's your to keep till the end of the world.'
His smile is a reflection of mine.
I'm finding the future in rhinestone.

Helen: At the Café

His green eyes are staring from the edge
astonished at this exotic bowl of fish.
He's silent – a sheet of glass
between him and me,
I want to shatter it – I sit with him.

…a smudge of jam on his cheek
his body hunched
hiding its gracefulness,
he avoids my look
in a blush of hasty panic.
There's a story in him
writhing, thrashing to the surface.
He's holding a rhinestone
shards of light like the flecks in his eyes.
I reach into his hiding place
with 'Tell me the story of your love.'

Michael

…a moment of terror
image devouring image
I'm numb with their reproach.
… his blue eyes swivel
with a madness I mistook for my own.
His questions shake the comfort
of all the studied thoughts around us,
a mad monk in Russia
a lab mouse running on an eternal wheel
but when I kissed him
to find an explosion in him
like shared bursts of laughter,
he swore at me, still beautiful.

All knowledge shrivelled into humdrum,
I fled to hide with my worried mother
trudging to job after tedious job
only seeing his blue eyes, the hair on his arms
replaying his laughter, his disgust with me.
I saw him with a girl and vomited
flesh and desire swirl then rot,
only one thing makes sense
words of gorgeous scepticism from another time,
I pick up a pen and howl…

Helen

Poetry – do you write it?
I can't write a word.
Each sentence rips before I…
You're gorgeous with your pen in hand
searching and blushing with each hesitation
then your eyes shine, finding your flow!
But there's something you want more!

Men are all around us
in uniforms, dresses, suits with loosened ties –
How they crave the power of a man
then his gentleness as he opens his body!
Dominance, submission, then back again.
So many come here to step from the shadows!
Ah those bruises on your neck!
Somebody's been loving you!
Wish I had just one of those!

Let me pour you a drink!
I have a house, a crumbling mansion
in a lively tree-lined street…

Michael

I've found a new mother
not with an apron,
cocooning me in safety
but in a fraying ball gown.
Wine overflows from our glasses
the fragrance of a joint back and forth,
she invites me to dance with her
in a world of wildness
where everything is reversed!
My body is alive, I pick up a pen
too dizzy to write!

The Breeze is Chilly: Michael's Poem to Vanessa

Away from you, the breeze is chilly.
Leaves are dying to yellow
leaping, then drift like idlers
posing questions like yours.

My ceiling is cracked but high.
The city spreads before me,
concrete towers like termite nests,
a place I've gracelessly given
endless reams of accounts
to the snap of grey folders,
framed rubber ducky on my desk.

Now Rimbaud opens next to Wilde
conversing like lunatics in smocks.

You lounge, wrapped in velvet.
Your purpled lips provoke me
tearing away the surface of my blandness,
the tightness of my strings unwound
into jousts of spontaneity.
Diamantes and gold leaf
mingle with crowded urinals,
gutter talk playfully refined.
New monsters thrill me
wrapped together from the street.

I take your lipstick
smear it on my mouth
like a drunken dandy.
We're searching for…
My feathers are my books
the distorting poison of their vision
the neon mixes with windswept meadows
and with you…

Lust

Sprawled in my chair
dizzying with each puff
my skin is purple
like the glowing fabric of my lamp,
beyond is only darkness.

I see Mozart
the whirling curves of his baton
powder sweating on his cheek.
I am now deaf
to the playful ease of his exuberance
too balanced, too perfect.
The needle screeches and jumps
as I squirm to see beyond
poetry smeared with ash on my desk
figurines of tarnished brass,
all the trappings of my cocoon.
Shadowy walls fall away to
knots of tangled energy
bare feet dancing, a quiver
through the calf's light down of hair
winking eyes, chins rough with bristles,
a kaleidoscope
of body parts hacked off whole.
Kissing lips close in to bite,
a golden face is smiling in the sun
as he whispers in my ear,
the smoothness of his chest spread wide
coaxing me to touch him.
I pick up a book, cast it aside
words frozen in patterns
laughing at my terror.
The music rises to delight.

My long-forgotten body
pinned by its timidity
starts to blossom lithe,
a precocious boy who always gets
I mouth the scrawlings from toilet walls
my erection urges
concentrating blood and spirit.
I button up my shirt
and search through chaos
for my lost shoes and socks.

At the Edge of Trees: Rushcutters Bay Park

At the edge of trees,
I cannot enter.
The moon illuminates
tense streaks of clouds
its rim peeps out
rusted with a filthy haze
full now but for a tiny bite
cut by fingers of branches
shaking with the wind
or with my terror and drunkenness.

All is quiet now but not still.
My flesh is alive
dreaming silhouettes of flesh
behind every lonely tree,
trunks rounded with leering bumps.

I wheel around, searching in panic
till I'm touched by a hand,
heated fingers play under my shirt
peeling at the coldness of my surface
tobacco breath tickles my ear
and as I turn
buttons flying from his shirt,
my cheek falls into the roughness of his chest
the glow of his skin
throbs with blood
touching my eyes, my tongue.
A wet scab on his knuckle
caresses my face.
I stand dizzy
in the chilly wind
not knowing how to channel
this bursting shock
as raindrops patter.
He pulls the clasp of my belt,
for a moment I am strong
until I giggle doubting it
buoyed by his choking, swallowing mouth.
He rises and stares
I fix into his eyes
I want my power again
I want his power
His hand touches my head…

2

The park now drains of urgency,
my buttocks squelch with mud
my trousers are undone
a bloody bite on my nipple from…
unshaven whiskey breath
bruises on scarred muscles
but beneath his roughened skin…
a pleading melted his threatening stance,
a demon in him leapt into me
a wild caress of my whole torso.
He pushed me away
when I asked his name…
Monsters have no name.
I lost my name
never again
the hush of my yawning suburb.
His heart beat as I licked his skin
our breath surged together,
is he changed into me,
an awkward stumbling boy with a book in his hand?
I stare at the shadows of men circling.
I feel a deep contentment.
I will never go back and hide.

Tony

The first light of dawn
reflects on the harbour.
I want to disappear.
I see him too
so awkward and ashamed
walking away.
A gang circles
men like me
shouting and stumbling
searching for the loners
broken bits of manhood,
we'll smash them together,
the degenerates, I'm crying
my head is bruised, knuckles bloody
bites on my neck,
his hair reflects the light
no scars like mine
will I kneel to him again
can he take away the fury?
Only in darkness.
I wave at the boys
roving for a fight,
I'm one of them.
My secret makes me stronger.
Where is she?
My twin, but stronger.
What is she doing now?

Helen

Are things really changing?
How well I remember
all my wandering
so much of it in chains and stifled!
I was pulling beers in a shady bar.
A few of the men see the scars in my eyes
gently squeezing my hand, a shared sigh.
Shy clerks come to life half singing the story
of beautiful bodies they touch in darkness,
the smell of sweat, a gasp of pleasure,
then police blow the whistle
a beating in a cell…
then a leap away to wild imagination…
A struggling Blanche is taken to the mad house
her eyes still flirtatious as Brando glowers
his shirt tight with muscles – ah I am her, you are him.
Callas howls as Tosca's kiss flashes
and Bette is smoking with burning eyes.

Then silence,
as we look at the world outside
simpering compliant women
stiff and constipated men, righteous in disgust,
meat pies, beer and cricket
rows of houses silent in the suburbs
races brothels and gangsters
but no love – it doesn't exist here.

Oh I had my men – huffing, everyday men
but they quickly fled from the sharpness of my tongue.
I treasure singularity
I rove within fantasies
seeking ways to demolish the normal.
But now – is freedom arriving?
I stumble, tears running down my cheeks.

Michael Finds a Gay Bar

1

A bar like the others
men encircle me
a love song reproaches
climbing ever upwards
as my thoughts dive in spite
to a blur of flesh.

They stand alone smoking
awkward in check shirts,
where's the flirtation
the teasing flamboyance?
I'm different – are they different like me?
Is this the place?
I search for a glint in revolving eyes
to read their longing
and write it on my body.

I want to strip beneath
the flowers on shirts, the stripes on ties
pursed lips, clenched arms –
are they drowning?
Which one of them can open me?
Tear at my painful oneness?

A stubbled drunk winks at me and staggers,
I see the sweetness of my body in his eyes.
Coloured lights flash
the singer fades
I scull a sickly sweetened rum
It burns down to my guts
charging my emptiness.
I want a lost boy,
tangled in fantasy
longing to speak
lips open for my kiss.

A glimpse is enough.
A spray of freckles,
his inward glance
suddenly bursting outwards.
Shadowed eyes soften and glow
hair flows to his shoulders,
my blurred wanting sharpens.
I'm shaking.

We stand mumbling
finding flaws, doubting
until he grasps my hand,
the smooth warmth of a body
touching mine, I'm alive.

2

We breath together in disbelief,
my gnawing hunger returning.
He whispers,
'Let's hold this moment.'
He scatters white powder
on Rimbaud's sneering face
as I search for a spoon.
The sting of a needle
I throw up
he comforts me,
no more anxiety,
we soothe our bodies in flowing kisses
no tearing as our climax holds,
the room is a meadow
the mess in my head is gorgeous.
When suddenly –
'Sorry, man, my girlfriend is waiting.'
and he's gone.
Love is a moment.
I'm a decadent at last.
I pick up a book.
I smell the lunch Helen is cooking
but I'm not hungry.

IV: Louise and Vanessa

A Café in Roslyn Street: Louise

I sit on the edge
as wide-eyed boys play guitar,
street girls wipe the purple from their lips.
Thoughts fly high
wrapped in sudden contagious laughter,
from long hair and spectacles
colourful bodies swivel and gesture
then a silence
but before I can speak
some new speculation glows
taking shape amongst them
so I listen
fearing the tremble of my voice
amongst people so unlike me
so comfortable in themselves.
A line of drunks stumble by exhausted
tied together like a chain gang.
Above in the darkest patch of night,
his finger slowly motions
his voice flat with certainty
'Come back. Who are these people?
You're not well, but I love you.
Let me explain the world to you.'
And just as I agree,
I see an orange slither in the sky
fresh dew in the wintry breeze…

2

Two rolling shrieks of delight!
She? Him? Her?
Mother and daughter? Lovers?
Feathers! Purple silk! Matching orange lipstick!
This unlikely couple gesture wildly
in the weird radiance of sunrise.
Have they escaped from some exotic book
to this café at the end of the world?
Others leap to greet them
but I look away,
wary of florid colour
in my world of mutters and sighs.
I choke on my cigarette
gasping with something as strange as laughter.
Quickly I look back.
She's beside me, offering her hand,
the lines on her face curve into a smile
then a beat, she's still –
I cover my face
the ugly stain of my bruises
I burst into tears
feeling worthless, so ashamed
until so gently, I feel her touch.
'You deserve better.'

I look between my fingers
at overdone make-up reddening her eyes,
a beauty spot on his/her youthful face
and now my lungs are tearing
again with the wildest laughter,
tears and snot drip from my nose
until I stop, embarrassed.
They're quiet now, smiling a gentle question,
their strangeness has a truth I want to find.
She hugs me, the young she hugs me
the warmth of their bodies and mine.
I wriggle free – I'm not ready for this.

'Do you have a place to stay?'
I say nothing, a moment of decision
like the day my husband proposed to me.
I shake my head and look at her.
'The sisterhood of the bruise.'
A burst of sunshine chases shadow away.
They're real, I'm shaking.
'I have a house,
a crumbling mansion
in a lively tree-lined street
a step away from this noise and anarchy…'

Louise at the Crumbling Mansion

Up the wooden staircase
panelled with mazes and question marks
to my very own room
the empty walls
peel red below green
mildewed shadows of torn down posters,
lost layers of eclectic taste
to which I want to add.
New books infect the old, scattered
on paint spattered floorboards.
Greer kisses George Eliot,
a chatter of flamboyant intellect
but I am silent.
I must know more
so my books can speak to me afresh,
as my mind repeats
his monotonous stare and his sigh.
My new friends are elsewhere,
not thinking of me…
Daring some disappointment,
I rise from my chair.
I wrap a colourful scarf
Helen gave me with laughter
around my throbbing head.
My agitation is promising.
The gargoyle smiles as I shut the gate.
Shadowy trees hint at shimmering greenness,
with shouts and guitars at my hearings edge.

Sweet Kisses and Brutishness

A minute away
the menagerie
let loose from their cages.
Toy soldiers from the suburbs
tear open the buttons of their shirts,
gyrating haywire.
This many-headed monster
draws me into its roaring beat,
as faces leer, circling for a mate
pausing and assessing.
I meet their stare,
too quirky and headstrong
to fit into their fantasy.
It's then the clawing inside me,
grows calm,
the chaos now surrounds me
I'm in its midst outside it.
My satiric eye is sharpened
as the city sheds its complacent skin.
A woman offers herself to all,
her eyes circle upwards to her brain
searching for a lost delight.
Two boys are laughing, calling her dog
they push her and she falls.
Is this a place to find yourself
or a glaring clifftop
they all leap from?

I help her to her feet
as a man drops beside her,
legs shake as he tries to right himself
frightened like a newborn foal.
The trauma I suffered is everywhere.

Old cynic with his bottle at the bank.
A fine mind thrusts with the darkness,
a swig of brandy to hold the vision
he sees it just like me-
a grotesque gallery in flux,
sweet kisses and brutishness
passing side by side
jostling for our future.
A boy sits beside him
holding a rhinestone.
Colours match the flecks in wide open eyes,
as his body quivers
with each detail of the street around us.
I look at it once more,
and remember why I came here,
to glimpse the new
in the blandness
of this meat and potatoes city.

Louise and Vanessa

1 Vanessa

As we walk, the street
reconfigures through your eyes-
you search beyond
the agitated surface –
all the bouncers thugs and drunks
I taunt and tittilate –
your brain burns with questions
like 'What is this?' and 'Why?'
you unsettle a shadow in me.
Whistles jolt your body,
bashful in the dress I gave
to stop you hiding in plainness,
as I blow a kiss and spin a pirouette.
You give a playful yawn
as you put your arm round my waist,
your cheek is on my shoulder.
I see the jagged nuance
you are seeing…

2 Louise

You close the door,
a refuge from the street
unravelling at dawn
glowing through your curtains,
its orange plays with the scarlet of your lamp
sequins twinkle in the brightness of your dresses,
singers levitate in posters on your wall,
as we droop in sweet exhaustion.

I open my mouth to speak,
your finger touches my lips
and then…
like we're whispering secrets…
at first I want to stop you…

you pull down the straps of your dress
and I gasp
your ribs breathing
through curving breasts
your taut smoothness full of warmth,
your penis dangles, a decoration
no pawing hands to push me down
just a cheeky smile – 'This is me,'
unique but nervous,
a work of strength, of transformation
asking for nothing, only telling
a searching back and forth,
your fingers on my zip.

I'm sitting in a chair
folding my arms
then as I unfold them,
I marvel at the fullness of my breasts.
All my fear is gone.
I return your thankful stare,
my body now open
in reflection with yours.
I feel my power,
you're still at last.
'You're beautiful.'

3 Vanessa

I gag playfully,
my finger in my mouth.
A woman so like me
so unlike me.
You look at me
through ever questioning eyes.
I feel myself shift,
no longer a gyrating doll
flapping in breezes like my dresses
but a woman strong in thinking.
Ideas quiver in your body.
You stare with fascination.
'I feel safe with you.'

4 Louise

Shadows flicker from the street.
The thugs are strutting, throwing punches.
You walk among them
teasing and provoking
but I can see your blush of fear,
they want to devour you, throw you aside.
You dare to go there, tell me what you see!
I'm tired of being frightened!
I want to tear beneath surfaces
right to this city's brutal heart!
In the safety of this vivid room,
let's tell our stories
let's find more strength than them!

I want to love my body again -
I love it now in your reflection.
I want to stand tall and speak.
I want us both to be safe!

5 Vanessa

I offer myself
in a way I never have before.
There's a sudden peel
of shared laughter
as I see my hurt
mirrored in your eyes.
We hug in peacefulness,
no writhing of desire.
Here is our refuge
from the world outside.

Louise to Helen

A green haze
of sunlight shaking through leaves,
footsteps and laughter
outside the window,
a shifting world,
so now I can be still.
I skip over the pages of my book
as I read the newness around me.
A woman can be…
I can be…

What is left within
after years besieged and scorned?
You drop a stone into darkness,
do you hear the faintest splash?
Helen always kept her fierceness,
a brightness lighting the pitch around her
her scorching humour
a mirror reversing the world.

Her hair is wild with flecks of grey.
Her voice resounds
as deep as her struggles.
She runs from the madhouse
spins in the streets of Soho
she nurtures lost elves,
she gathers memories
in her cloaks, rings and brooches.
She winks.
'Our battles are not over.
Together we're strong!'

As we drink,
she flips over my sighs,
all my missteps change
to discoveries
the many layers of a complex woman.
A wise woman, a virago.
She gives me a new scarf
as she starts on another story.

Louise to Michael

Dylan is insisting,
his voice tangles with yours and mine,
you replace the needle again and again –
who better to sing with
than him – and you?

Your eyes are green,
they never stop wondering,
pulsing bright
from a darkness at their edge,
gentle boy
in this world of men who hurt,
squirming with delight
on your wine-stained couch,
your story leaping over violins
in pungent smoke rings
as poets cough out lines
from open pages on the dusty carpet.
You pick up records, fling them aside.
Silver stems of your candelabra
flicker and rotate,
our senses disarranged,
the delicate skin of your neck
stained with blood-tinged bruises.
The music stops,
we collapse together
in gasps of painful laughter
then as you search for another record…

…they hem you in,
a circle of pimply, spitting schoolboys,
you share my panic
as my husband stares,
a polished table, a crystal glass
the room at last impeccable
my shoulders hunched from vacuuming
but he's still furious
sensing the static in my brain.
You look up at me with a blushing smile.
I see you lonely in the park
your love is gagged
hidden in darkness and danger,
it's time to move it into light!
Outside our home
thugs line up in dishevelled suits,
ready to hurl us off the cliff.
Their master is wrapped in guns and banknotes.
Or can we infect them with our thoughts?
You pick up a pen, laughing loudly,
how can you distil these images?
I want to write these truths around us
in resounding prose for everyone.
I want…
but you are snoring,
and I curl up beside you.

Sydney Tribune, 12 October 1973.
Save the Terraces on Victoria Street!
by Louise Healey

Historic terraces in Victoria Street are under threat of demolition! A greedy property developer wants to replace them with high-rise apartments. The fabric of the area, built up over decades, will be destroyed.

These terraces are a community of older people, single people, artists and writers who cannot afford to live elsewhere. Every city needs its place where new ideas are exchanged, where new fashions begin. Victoria Street is a vibrant place where people come to discover themselves and change. That energy is gone if you evict them and scatter them. A strand of the city's creativity will be smashed. Any new apartments will be bought by well-off people who can afford to live anywhere.

Shady gangsters and corrupt cops are trying to drive the residents out. They are paid by a notorious criminal identity who runs pubs and brothels in Kings Cross. They've formed an alliance to get control of the buildings. The residents face daily threats and intimidation. Support the Green Bans! Support Jack Mundey! Support Juanita Neilsen! Save Victoria Street!

V: After Dinner

Helen

A hot needle threads in my brain,
a kiss of Vanessa's lipstick
or is it mine?
on the rim of my last crystal glass
its delicacy cracked,
and yes! A heart-starting quaff
of red – saved just for me.
It moves from the parch of my tongue
with a kick right through me
The world around me now clear –
in its chaos.

A twisted roach
blackened with tar
near an overturned ashtray!
I rasp, dizzy with its poison,
fragments of last night are squirming –

…sweet flesh of cherry –
Michael pitted their stones
stealing a bite, dribbling scarlet.
Vanessa squeezes orange tang
on the duck's fat flesh,
Louise chops and dices
coiled leaks, wizened face of artichoke,
it all emerges on a platter,
a field of flowers, tender flesh…

but now there's nothing but
oozing shards of fat
on the mismatched plates
I rescued from some dumpster.
Gnawed piles of bones
flung around the carpet,
Brussels sprouts, head of broccoli
garlic charred on rosemary sprig,
I take a flavoursome lick.
I smack my lips
like a dead duck's quack.
Did we conjure a taste of Paris
in this meat and potatoes city?

…black grooves of vinyl
smudged with treacle and cream
glow in the nauseating midday sun.
I draw the moth-eaten curtains,
scorching tip of joint in my mouth.
What a night! I remember…

…as Vanessa lip synchs
Callas's mad scene,
driving us crazy, howling warped together!
Louise's raucous laughter
as she whispers in my ear,
'I love Vanessa, I love you, I love…'

Michael leaps around her
as a drunken Russian faun
gyrating to the Rite of Spring
a flower in his hair,
freed from the leg iron of thwarted love.

They work their magic on each other –
I've created something!
Me! Who can't write a word!
Cherry, orange, garlic, duck –
simmer the flavours together
to make something delicious.
Throw four yearning people
together in this crumbling mansion
our bruises fall away,
we are transformed!

Suddenly…

…staccato shouting
boots stamp then halt,
all colour drains from the street
to a black and white newsreel
of thugs standing in line
about to spit in our faces.

A barking of orders,
a drumroll of running feet
muffles rising shrieks,
the thwack of an axe
pierces the panelling
destroying the door,
a shaking howl
as they enter our neighbour's house.

It's on.
Just as I always dreaded.
Just hours ago the street was alight
with our laughter and music!
Oh God!
A belting on the door,
like a summons to hell.
Will they drag us libertines
to a freezing wasteland?

Helen to Tony

It's just Tony and a mate.
I know him.
I like him.
I say hello, he smiles back
whenever I see his shambling vigour
in the street, up to no good.

He stammers.
I see an aching neediness
he struggles to hide,
he has the urgency
of an awkward young movie star.
He shadows Vanessa,
a muscular overgrown puppy,
squealing as he wags his tail,
rolling on his hairy tummy to be stroked.
He's the kind of man I could always soothe,
he could come to me for a makeover
anytime – oh to channel his jagged energy!

His smile flickers when he sees it's me
but quickly, it's erased.
His mate rests an iron bar on his shoulder.
'Why don't you both come in for a drink?'
Tony's lively face, nicely spoiled by a scar
drains to a grim mask,
he's received his command,
he must slice any quiver of questioning
from his brain.
All that's left is the bland face of a killer,
an extension of his bloodthirsty master.
He cackles.

And yet –
we had a complicity –
how to reach for it again?

…until Vanessa appears.
He blushes and fidgets,
dropping his eyes
fingering a truncheon
the bulge of his gun,
he's beautiful again.
He stammers 'Y…y…you?'
'D…don't hurt my friends, Tony.'
She stutters too!
Michael appears and gasps.
Tony lets out a wail.
Michael holds out his hand.
Vanessa giggles uncontrollably.
Louise is amazed, then she gets it.
We're standing together.
We link hands.
We know him better than he knows himself.
'Join us!'
There's a power
in the room's lively chaos
the brightness of the walls,
the strident optimism of posters
calling for FREEDOM! EQUALITY!
the scattered remains of our lavish banquet
but most of all, a power in us.
We blossom
with months of self-discovery and laughter.
'Join us, Tony!'

His mate moves forward.
He follows.
Not to embrace us.
They rip at the posters.
They smash a gathering
of my wooden saints, sea shells, erotic porcelain figures –
all my cherished baubles –
with their bludgeons.
Then Tony runs at us,
eyes drained to deadliness
but his mate says
'Enough!'
Tony retreats like a robot.
'Be out of here tomorrow,'
says the mate, and they leave.
More crashes and screeching in the street.
Vanessa gets up to follow him,
but stops.
We fall into a sobbing huddle.

Sydney Tribune, 8 January 1974
Outrage!
by Louise Healey

The residents of Victoria Street have been illegally evicted!

On 4 January 1974, a group of thugs paid by a notorious Kings Cross gangster attacked the community of Victoria Street. They were backed by squads of Police. Doors and windows were smashed with iron bars, residents were violently ejected from their homes. The living rooms, their furnishings, books and paintings were trashed. They've been living peacefully together for years, they have nowhere to go, a few have been offered housing near Blacktown.

There's a sinister alliance between Police, politicians, property developers and gangsters in this state. We're at a cross roads. Sterile developments only for the rich, or our vibrant, creative inner city communities…

೫೦೩

Terrania Creek Revisited

The gigantic trunk towers
with guts on the outside,
tangled tentacles and vines
burrow under rock stubbled with moss
reaching greedily for the creek's trickle.
Buttresses splay outwards
grey lizard skin,
turquoise lichen swirls
in a pattern that never holds
it cracks and flakes beneath my finger.
I sit on a fallen trunk,
gnarled with twisting lines.
I crane my neck, dizzy
as branches reach, splitting away
in light shifting from grey
to golden then scorching white.

Leaves above quiver, almost still
a metallic greenness.
Fern fronds are yellow streaked
drooping at their tips.
The trunk is dry
no squelch of rotting wood
the soil is still black
but powders in my fingers.
Dead leaves blow
disintegrating.
All is calm, waiting for…

It's a beloved face
brown eyes opaque
shadowed with tiny lines
looking into itself.
The body still vigorous
but at rest,
no sparking of action,
no sudden laughter
no surreal flurry of stories
like fresh leaves shaking in the sun
the chime of birds hovering, landing then scurrying
the rushing and bubbling of the creek.
Instead a sigh
a fraying at the edges
as a breeze begins to blow.

After the Bushfire
(Bells Line of Road)

Twisting boughs are shadows
against a grey and misty sky.
The ground is bleached and naked
except for shrivelled leaves
twigs like bones
raked from a furnace
tufts of burnt grass
crunch under my boots.
Still the tree stands
a husk
its pitted furrowed trunk
crumbles when I touch it
hollow dry and drained,
black, just blackness
and whitened ash under foot.

A thriving canopy
mottled trunks oozing with moss
tangled with fern fronds and shrubs,
all wither as the air is sucked away
then blown back in a scorching bellow.
As the whirlpool takes hold
shattering and flashing,
boiling sap bursts
leaves budding and opening
in years of slow sunlight
crackle and explode in a moment.

A roar of blinding orange
scours and leaps high
hurling up particles of ash
which seethe and gather
into choking palls of smoke,
blocking out the sun
to make a smouldering dusk of midday,
a stinking remnant of the forest's life
blows round the country, round the world.

Regeneration

Juice from a vein
feeds a clump of petals
dotted with magnifying raindrops,
but it's not a bouquet
pinned to the crumbling tar
of a sarcophagus
in a graveyard of trees.
It's a fresh twig
shining ripe purple
with clusters of leaves
budding in mauve
then sparkling in a nursery green,
blowing in the drizzly breeze.

The twigs are multiplying
in the split of a bough,
a ravaged black armpit
sprouts thriving colours.
The trunk is ripped open
a black hollow cave,
the roots are puckered and bubbled,
a broken sculpture
drained of life
but now the corpse is twitching.

In this upside down forest,
new born sprays of leaves
shoot from the trunks
and upwards in sleeves
over blackened boughs.
The twigs at the top are bare,
tips wagging in the breeze.
Scorched bark peels away
to layers of blasted wood,
as the tree's white heart
is revealed in patches,
now festooned with leaves
over scars shining with raindrops.

The clouds shift and darken.
The trees descend into the valley
merging into a mourning grey,
slowly disappearing in mist.
The rain starts pelting.

Rain at Rosebank

The sky thickens
tissues of grey
sliced with fissures of white,
a fleshy cortex
stained with purple blotches
fattening to burst
from its membrane
as the sun's twisting feelers glow.

A splash on my cheek,
sodden leaves are shaking in the wind.
The valley's starving yellow
bursts with muddy pools and streams.
The rain cascades
it rolls through germinating grass,
a blur of misty grey
as the clouds open wide.
I am drenched.
But I stay,
my flesh blushes and tingles
startled by new desires.

Coachwood Glen

for Peter Urquhart on his 40th birthday

Silence, almost silence.
The creek trickles
hairs of a bow vibrating on rock.
The looming roughness of the cliff above
glows between cracks in the leaves.

Silence, then a chime,
warm and embodied,
three notes playfully repeating.
My gasp rises –

So sudden in swiftness,
it lands on a log.
Feathers ruffle,
darting beak preens.

Black eyes glint
from a yellow stripe,
another lands, then another,
the first shoots up to the leaves.

Silence, moistness,
translucent canopy –
I wait again for song.

2 Moss

Leaves flutter like my thoughts
up in the dizzy canopy.
I want to slow to a

stillness in the shadows,
the stump of a giant tree
standing broken in shade

flickering with sunlight
squeezing through the branches.
Its bark is shrouded in moss.

Distorted fingers dig into earth
roots wrapped in moss like a stocking
laddered and torn
with gnarls and brown splinters.

Not one moss, but mosses
bandaged upwards on the trunk.
My eyes dig deeper to

clusters of stems with minuscule leaves
or a fine down of bristles
magnified by sparkling droplets

tiny brushes with a
seed of jade at the top,
rough like fluff to the touch.

Loops of rotting rug
cling to furrows still pitted on the trunk
to muscular curves of roots.

Tribes of mosses jostle thicken prosper,
a sodden surface of precocious green
darkening to veins of black-tinged emerald.

It's only a mask,
it crumples
as I prod beneath,

tightly wound splinters unravel
to a stringy white mulch
rich in trapped sap.

The moss enjoys its slow banquet
feeding on splashes of sunshine
as leaves flutter in the glowing canopy.

3

The trees cascade
down jagged rocks
in giant strides
to the hidden creek
rippling through the chasm
as branches split and lift up
waving leaves to my eyes.
The sun beats white holes in the clouds.

Faraway
at the tip of a branch
flashes of bronze
speckles of sunrise
ripening to gleeful greenness
trembling down the twigs.
Like a dancer
letting their colourful tresses fly,
feet firmly planted below as
a shaking rises from their core
merging with the breeze
in an ancient ritual
full of springtime spontaneity.

Then the wind stops
the leaves are frozen
in a scale of colours
like flecks of thread
woven into an antique carpet
a craft refined for generations.

Branches twist
into the bending of boughs
crooked curves multiply
with demented logic
like an abstract artist
channelling the grooves of his brain
into his tearaway brush
a suite of works on one subject
all vastly different.
Branches diminish
budding with twigs
waving with leaves.

Bark peels from the trunk
strands of old wallpaper
shrivelling in strips
to reveal a weathered marble column
stained by the centuries.
A tree grounded in the valley
thrusting itself upward above the canopy.

Echidna

Now the roughness of rock
mottled with rust
sprouts twigs eaten by a lichen clump,
and above, a single purple flower.
then I shift…

…like a slap to my vision,
dark fur inhales
pierced with thorns
beak shifting in the grass…

My mouth opens –
I find the word
from a moment of childish astonishment.

Details grow as I breathe,
yellow quills taper to prickles
from a down of black-tinged brown,
so vulnerable,
it puffs into a ball

and I know I have a second
to let this clash of weird unlikeliness
blend into a harmony
like a purple flower on a jagged rock,
so immediate in its quivering life.

As I shift closer
its needles jolt.
It sways to the shadow of bushes
spangled with tiny white flowers.

Later when I see my friend
knowing he loves the unlikely wondrous,
I bounce the word high
'I saw an echidna. An ECHIDNA!'
and blurt a jumbled rush of this poem.

Banksia

I am disquieted,
walking down the ridge.
Like always I see
wild clumps of flowers
towering tree trunks
pretty birds flit,
but sweetness brings no solace.
I cannot connect.
It's just well drawn pictures
on some wall faraway.
Then I see –
Grey bristles thickly layered
on broken curves,
a scattering of misshapen heads.
Each profile
differs in its shrunken roughness.
They are unmoving,
while freshly green gum leaves
shake in the feeble breeze.
At last I can focus –
on banksia cones,
as they draw me more deeply
into their grotesquely poised stillness.
Their broken teeth
are half spat out,
poking from the stubble.
Their faces have no centre –
without eyes, but their many mouths
are smooth and hard as molluscs.

They're fringed by leaves
mottled and serrated
blistered with lumps,
their sharp edges rusted.
Limbs jut out
at ever more unlikely angles
from a short fat trunk.
Branches thicken and twist,
their bark fissured rough
speckled with lichen.
I touch the undulating bumps,
breaking off moist black specks…

…Nanna! Tell it once more! Please!
My grandmother's gleeful,
she's propped up with pillows.
Her voice is thick with fantasy.
And he pounced!
The goblin banksia man!
I pass the story on
delighted nephews scream.

I want you still
to spring to life,
quickened by some ancient
hybrid spirit
half human and half reptile.
At home with diprotodons
thylacines and giant kangaroos
whose muscular arms reach
and tear down whole trees for fruit.

The Gundangara are hunting,
telling your story with love.
While you wait for fire
lizard banksia man,
to destroy all else around
so you can drop your waiting seeds
and breed.

Albarracin Fantasia

to Marguerite Montes

A dry wind blows
through a narrow lane way.
Homes cluster, rendered orange
with the soil of arid fields.
An open door,
vine leaves with purple flowers
climb in a shady courtyard.
A steeple rises
bleaching white
in the blue glare of the sun
tickling and burning my skin
wet with sweat.
The tower's rounded symmetry
is dwarfed
by jagged pinnacles
hewn by glaciers and storms,
rocky cliffs plunging
down in jolts
to cool pools of a river.

Thick grasses greedily drink
at the bottom of the valley,
a grove of cypresses shelters me
branches droop
thick with green needles.
The town is clenched to the mountain,
its rock tamed into bouldered houses,
an ancient church next to the everlasting.

Walls to keep out some forgotten enemy
become a haven from the harshness
they were built from.

Water trickles like guitar notes,
and in the fading summer twilight
the ghost of El Greco's Jesus stands firm
straddling the mountains
casting his yearning eyes aloft
then a singer's voice deep with a song of desire.

Altarpiece Saint Mary's Krakow

Golden robes are filling with breath,
eleven men and a woman
in a twilight of darkening blue.
A finger wildly points above,
they stare upwards, at each other
vigorous men in turmoil,
handsome with their flowing curls
well kept beards, all certainty shaken
bewildered by the inexplicable.
One searches a book for the answer
one presses his hands to hold something precious
as a woman prays in devastation.
They are bursting into three dimensions
like a chorus singing to different tunes,
because they sense them still, but cannot see them –
a man and a woman hover above,
in tranquil stillness as angels flutter…

My mouth moves in a shifting prayer,
my hand shakes –
I want to light a candle
to a friend back home,
exhausted by chemotherapy
to another friend, torn by surgery
to a shy Polish boy
smiling after I kissed him –
can I pray for them here?
A place that crushes our love?

I see men in Warsaw wrapped in flags
brandishing a crucifix
and the deep shame of Auschwitz, a short drive away.

I am bewildered.
Flocks of winged Cupids
swoop then nestle
on swirling patterns etched in columns
curving upwards to the golden dome.
Stained-glass windows
fracture the spring sunshine –
stories vivid in shards of purple, red and green
golden stars sparkle
in sky-blue darkening to an ocean.

The figures are awkward with longing,
in a twilight where everything shifts,
remembering a man
who shocked them into love.
My head is swivelling like theirs,
as piece after lovingly crafted piece
shifts me into the extraordinary.

Are they the craftsmen
sketched by the artist as they worked
or chatting on a break,
perplexed by the world's confusion?
One tints a glass fragment,
one carves the lithe body
of an angel with butterfly wings
one chisels a pattern searching inward
another coats it with gold,
another with blue.
They do not forget friends' deaths
plague and endless wars
the hotheads trumpeting their hate
but they channel their energy –
together, they create.
I light my candle.

Warsaw Square

The sky is purple
cut by the clock tower.
Neon labels blaze.
Lively couples rove,
but there's a hint
in twilight shadows
of a city smashed to rubble.

When…
They swagger towards me
wrapped in red and white flags,
clustered in a pack,
old scars reopen, stinging.
One brandishes a falanga –
a crucifix cut with a sickle.
A red flare shoots, smoking the sky.
Banners and placards
easy to translate
three word slogans
threadbare with shrillness,
secret mutters now shouting in public,
the bullies are back,
they're out and proud.

I clench my arms
holding my thoughts
fearing they will see them,
like a boy frightened
to board a school bus.

I shiver
in this cheerful spring time night –
will they encircle me, push me between them,
a gobbet of spit, a flurry of punches
to break me,
make me follow
like an echo in their pack?

I want to leap into their path
flamboyant
my voice rising in eagerness
as I share an unexpected moment of beauty,
diamantes on my cape of clashing colours,
a smear of lipstick,
they'll fall silent in amazement,
or a hidden waverer will step out of line,
searching for the path to eccentricity –
I'll walk away, holding his hand…

I clench my arms,
hiding my thoughts.

Warsaw Gay Bar

A circling ball
brushes searching faces, gesturing bodies
with splashes of green and purple,
a singer taunts us with her purring.
I see you mouth the words
with trouble shining in your eyes
to no one in particular.

I'm next to you now,
your hair curls like a hungover Chopin
smokes leaks from your lips as you smirk,
I take your cigarette
tasting your spittle.
You stand awkward
as if your pulsing desire
leaves you open
to the street's barely hidden violence,
is anywhere safe from hurt?
I speak, but you do not hear my words,
but read them in my body,
'You're what I want.'
My wandering hand
plays with the breath in your back
our rippling anxiety slows
your lips now a thankful smile
reflecting mine.
Your tongue is brackish with booze,
I drink it in
we're swirling in multicoloured light.

To Candy Royalle

You quiver with energy
the audience hush
waiting for your poem.

Your tenderness, your breath
clash with the unspeakable,
the lies that corrode us

the massacres
words like their guns
reveal to us the killing fields

the bullets now our apathy.
You search the smoking debris
for what is left…

a cherished shape
writhing with desire
in a battle of kisses…

Now your body fills the room
to take on cops
kicking kooris to the ground

or that monstrous grin
in a speckled sky – death.
the audience are a single breath

in silence as you pause
gathering to a cheer, a roar
something has shifted…

Notes

'Forest Elegy' – inspired by the Protestor's Falls Walk near the Channon Northern New South Wales.

'Essay on Shakespeare' – *Macbeth* Lady Macbeth Act 1, Sonnet 29, *Henry 6* part 3 Act 5 Gloucester, Sonnet 20.

'Amber Hand's – with thanks to ABBA and the Beatles for echoes of lyrics, *Richard 3* Act 1 Gloucester.

'A Cold Sweat on the Lawn' – thanks to St Paul's College Oval University of Sydney.

'First Impressions' – contains a paraphrase from Victor Sheehan *Time Needs a Tyre Change*.

'I Am Not Dostoevsky' – inspired by *Notes from Underground*, *The Brothers Karamazov* and Rachmaninoff's Piano Concerto No. 3

'Endgame' – with thanks to Endgame Samuel Becket, also paraphrase of Arthur Rimbaud 'The Drunken Boat', 'Season from Hell'.

'Nightclub' – with thanks to Annie Lennox, Donna Summer, *Richard 3* Act I. The lyrics are remembered echoes, not quotes.

'Another Walk' – 'the Wall' a place for male prostitution and The Sacred Heart Hospice where many people died of AIDs are opposite each other in Darlinghurst Road Darlinghurst.

'Fearsome passageway' is a paraphrase from the *Tibetan Book of the Dead*.

'Trickster Spirit' – the intersection of Taylor Square Darlinghurst had a lot more traffic before the Eastern Distributor. There was a patch of grass in the middle with a single palm tree called Gilligan's Island. Many pubs and nightclubs were nearby. Victor sometimes enjoyed drawing people as half animal half human.

'Performance' – this contains paraphrases from Victor Sheehan's plays *Time Needs a Tyre Change*, performed at the University of Sydney 1985, *Deadflat Saga* performed at Jellyheads 1992 and *Flower to Furnace*, performed at the Wayside Chapel 1996. I did not put in quotes, rather phrases and ideas that echoed in my mind from when I learned the lines years ago. I wanted the work to be mine rather than his. With thanks and prayers for Victor Sheehan (1957–2017). The plays have been donated to the State Library of NSW. He has no blood heirs. I am his literary heir.

'The Captain' – partly inspired by Victor Sheehan's play *Mecca of Misfits,* performed at the Gearco Warehouse 1993.

'Victoria Street Helen' – inspired by the protests in Victoria Street Kings Cross 1973–4.

Juanita Neilsen was murdered in 1974. Helen and all the other characters are fictitious.

Earlier versions of a few of the poems in 'Victoria Street: A Kings Cross Fantasia' were published in my previous book *Dining at the Edge*, also available from Ginninderra Press. They are 'Louise in the Suburbs', 'Michael in the Suburbs', 'Michael on Darlinghurst Road', 'Car Job', 'Tony and the Boss', 'Vanessa's Love Song', 'Reflections in Rhinestone' and 'A Café in Roslyn Street' part 1.

'Michael in the Suburbs' – thanks to Bob Dylan.

'Michael on Darlinghurst Road' – inspired by the neon signs for Porky's and the Pink Pussy Cat, both strip clubs.

'Tony and the Boss at the Venus Room' – 'The Boss' is inspired by the late Jim Anderson who managed many Kings Cross venues including the Venus Room and *Les Girls* in the 1970s.

'Vanessa and Shirley at *Les Girls*' – *Les Girls* was a cabaret for drag performers from the mid-sixties to the early 90s. Shirley Bassey was a favourite singer for many of the artists, especially her hit 'This is My Life'.

'The Breeze is Chilly' – written in the style of Michael Dransfield with love.

'At the Edge of Trees' – the western edge of Rushcutters Bay Park was and still is a notorious gay beat. It had more trees and less lighting in the 1970s.

'Helen' – with thanks to Tennessee Williams *Streetcar Named Desire*, Puccini *Tosca* and Bette Davis *All About Eve*. Tosca's kiss is the knife with which she stabbed Scarpia.

'After the Bushfire' – in memory of the summer 2019/2020 bushfires which devastated the Blue Mountains near Blackheath and the Bells Line of Road.

'Coachwood Glen' – this a walk starting on the Megalong Road near Blackheath.

'Albarracin Fantasia' – Albarracin is a walled town in Teruel province Spain.

'Warsaw Gay Bar' – thanks to Amy Winehouse.

'To Candy Royalle' – Candy's fabulous book *A Trillion Tiny Awakenings* is available from UWAP Press. She was the queen of Sydney's performance poetry scene.

Previous publications: thanks to *Plumwood Mountain* for parts of 'Forest Elegy', *Sappho Anthology 2021* for 'My Clown' and 'Maze', *Urban Village* for 'Vanessa and Shirley at Les Girls', Ginninderra Press *Mountain Secrets* for 'Coachwood Glen 1', *Poetry Sydney* for 'Essay on Shakespeare' and *Sydney to Bistrita* for 'Endgame'.

About the Author

Charles Freyberg is a Kings Cross (Sydney) poet and playwright. In the 1990s he worked as an actor and director, especially with the surreal clown Victor Sheehan, his first poetic mentor. His own writing started with drag shows and performance art staged at Club Bent at the Performance Space in the late nineties, and with a number of plays. He studied poetry at postgraduate level at the University of Sydney, supervised by Judith Beveridge. His poems have been published in *Meanjin*, *Plumwood Mountain*, the Poetry Sydney website and Ginninderra Press's *Mountain Secrets* anthology. His first book *Dining at the Edge* is also published by Ginninderra Press. His work has been widely performed, including in Peter Urquhart's the *Experiment* at the Sydney Conservatorium, *Vanessa and Friends* a theatrical night of his poetry at El Roco in Kings Cross, at *Museum of Fleas* with the Sydney Fringe, *Taken for a Ride* with the Surry Hills Festival and the Nimbin Poetry World Cup. He received an award for his services to LGBQI poetry at the National Art School during Mardi Gras 2020. He is often heard at Sydney performance poetry gigs, including Word in Hand, Caravan Slam, Glebe Poetry Lounge, Live Poets at Don Bank and Poetica Bondi. Charles has turned a selection of poems from *The Crumbling Mansion* into a one-person show which may come to a venue near you. He gives thanks to all the beautiful enlivening eccentrics who have inspired him. The image of Charles was drawn by Tristan Franki in 1986, the time of the Victor poems.

www.ingramcontent.com/pod-product-compliance
Lightning Source LLC
Chambersburg PA
CBHW070901080526
44589CB00013B/1162